#WRITERS911

#WRITERS911

How to Tackle Writer's Block & Unleash Your Creativity!

ELLEN POTTER

Tiggy House Books

Copyright © 2020 by Ellen Potter

All rights reserved.

ISBN-13: 978-1-7360757-4-6 (paperback edition)

ISBN-13: 978-1-7360757-3-9 (e-book edition)

No part of this book may be reproduced in any form or by any electronic or mechanical means, including information storage and retrieval systems, without written permission from the author, except for the use of brief quotations in a book review.

Artwork from Adobe/Strichfiguren.de

Cover images from Canva

For every writer who's ever felt hopelessly stuck. So, yeah . . . for every writer.

Contents

#Writer911	ix
Introduction	xi
STUCK IN THE BEGINNING	xiii
1. #SelfDoubt	1
2. #StoryIdeas	5
3. #TooManyIdeas!	11
4. #NoTimeToWrite	15
5. #MyIdeasStink!	19
6. #CreatingGreatCharacters	23
7. #FantasyWorldBuilding	28
8. #Who'sTellingTheStory?	33
9. #Research	41
10. #ShouldIWrite2Stories@Once?	55
11. #NamingCharacters	57
12. #TheAntihero	63
13. #ReadyToWriteANovel?	67
14. #PenOrComputer?	71
15. #WritingPartners	75
16. #WritingRoutine	80
17. #Collaboration	86
STUCK IN THE MIDDLE	91
18. #Can'tStopProcrastinating	92
19. #ImaginationFail	95
20. #Perfectionism	100
21. #MyCharactersFeelBlah!	104
22. #InternetDistraction!	108
23. #StuckAgain!What'sWrongWithMe?	113
24. #Copycat	117
25. #BoredOfMyStory	122
26. #Secrets&Lies	127
27. #FreakyFactor	131
28. #MessyPlot	135

STUCK AT THE END	141
29. #UnfinishedStories	142
30. #WhatWillPeopleThink?!	146
31. #TheEnd?	149
32. #OuchCriticism!	153
33. #Rejection	156
34. #Revision	163
35. #TechTalk	168
36. #BestJobsForWriters	174
37. #GettingPublished	178
38. #DIYWritingWorkshop	185
39. #Top10WritingTips	191
40. #Writers911!	193
About the Author	201
Also by Ellen Potter	203

#Writer911

HOW TO TACKLE WRITER'S BLOCK & UNLEASH YOUR CREATIVITY!

by Ellen Potter

Introduction

Okay, I'm going to tell you a secret. Ready?

Every single time I sit down to write one of my books, I get desperately, horribly, hopelessly stuck.

Every single time.

When I'm stuck, it feels as though I've driven into a muddy ditch and no matter how much I step on the gas, I can't move. My wheels are just spinning and spinning. It's an awful, frustrating feeling. So what's the first thing I do when I'm stuck? Heads up, I'm not proud of this. The first thing I usually do is go online to see which celebrity did something ridiculous that day. Oh, and then I might remember that there is some leftover blueberry pie in the fridge. Yeah, that's got to be polished off. And then I'll check my emails. About a thousand times.

In the end, though, I always manage to haul myself out of that mud and finish my book. Is it because I was born with an extra helping of will power? Not at all. It's because I have a whole stash of "Stuckbusters." What are Stuckbusters? They're simple tools and strategies that give me the traction I need to get my story moving again.

Introduction

In this book, I'm going to show you how to zap your inner critics, how to put procrastination into a chokehold, and how to duck and dodge frustration like a pro. By the time you're done reading this, you will have some serious stuckbusting skills!

Ready?

Let's do this.

STUCK IN THE BEGINNING

ONE

#SelfDoubt

Even though I'm a published author, I still worry that I'm not smart enough or talented enough to be a writer. While I'm writing, I often hear this sneering voice in my head. It says, "Um, excuse me. Just what do you think you're doing? You barely passed high school chemistry and you're trying to write a *book*?! Ha! Good luck, Loser!"

I call this voice The Mean Girl, and believe me, it's a hard voice to ignore. Especially since I really did barely pass high school chemistry.

I think a lot of people feel that they aren't smart enough or talented enough to be a writer. The Mean Girl (whom you might experience as The Snarky Guy or The Mocking Family Member) loves to hang around people like us. She'll sit on our lap, snapping her gum and yammering on and on about all the ways we are not good enough.

How do we get rid of her? I'm not going to lie to you. She doesn't scare easily. Even if you manage to push her off your lap, she'll probably come circling back again. She may even hang around you for your entire life. Below are a few things you can do to weaken her power over you.

Stuckbusters

- If the Mean Girl tells you that you're not smart enough to be a writer, remind her that most writers aren't geniuses. Plenty of successful writers struggled while they were in school. I certainly did. Being a good fiction writer is about your ability to create dynamic characters, not your ability to recite the periodic table. Sure, you may be able to impress readers with your knowledge of Gamma Ray astronomy, but if you can't make them care about the girl gazing though the telescope, they are going to toss your story aside

- Remember, fiction writing is not about *you* and how smart or talented you are. Fiction writing is about your characters. Your job as a writer is to help your characters navigate through the world you've created for them, to help them work through their dilemmas, to watch them connect or fail to connect with other characters. If your friend called you on the phone, sobbing, would you say, "Sorry, I'm not smart enough to help you," and then hang up? Of course not. You'd talk your friend through it. Do the same for your characters. Immerse yourself in their dramas, not your own.

- Despite all your best efforts, that Mean Girl may still be hanging around. I told you she was hard to get rid of! Take a cool, logical approach. When the Mean Girl has just about convinced you that you have the literary skills of a hermit crab, it's time to produce your body of evidence. In the beginning, the evidence might be pretty slim—one really good short story that you wrote last summer, a great descriptive sentence, or even a well-written e-mail. This is your proof that you do have the ability to write. The more you write, the heftier your body of evidence will grow, making it harder for the Mean Girl to convince you that you can't write. My body of evidence used to fit in a manila folder. Now it is spilling out of my bookshelves in the form of author copies, filling closets and generally annoying my family. But you know what? I need that evidence. Even after writing twenty books, I still need to prove to myself that yes, indeed, I can actually write. Take that, Mean Girl!

TWO

#StoryIdeas
___

Sometimes a good story idea will just drop into your lap unexpectedly. For instance, while sitting in a cafe, you overhear a conversation about a burglar who got stuck in a chimney, and he turned out to be the homeowner's high school prom date. *Blam!* There's a story idea. I call that "Writer's Swag" because it's the universe handing you an idea freebie. The thing is, you can't wait for Writer's Swag in order to begin writing. It could be years before some juicy idea lands in your lap. You have to seek out ideas if you want to write more than one story every decade or so.

Luckily, great ideas hide in plain sight. A while back, I took my son and his friends to the beach to look for sea glass. At first they were bummed because they couldn't find any. "There's nothing here," one boy said. "Let's try another beach." But then one of them found a little green sliver of sea glass. Soon after that, the rest of the kids started finding sea glass too. There were dozens of shards of amber, green, and white sea glass scattered among the rocks. Once the kids really started to look, the sea glass was everywhere! That's how story ideas are too. They are literally all around you. In order to see them, you need to *want* to see them.

Oh, and keep a notebook or a note-taking app nearby and write down those ideas when you spot them. You might think you would never forget such a great idea, but trust me, ideas have a way of sneaking off if you don't capture them in writing.

Below are hiding places where you might find intriguing story ideas. And remember, they're *hiding* places, which means you have to do some seeking.

Idea Hiding Places

- **Memories**. Many of my book ideas were sparked by childhood memories. I took those memories and shaped them into something new. For instance, when I was a kid my older brother was bullied pretty badly in school. He was super smart (still is) and instead of fighting the bullies with his fists, he fought them with his brains. One time, this kid was stealing Oreos from my brother's lunch every day. My brother knew who was stealing the cookies, but this kid was so mean that if my brother confronted him, he would definitely get the snot beaten out of him. So my brother used his brains to solve the problem. At home he took out three Oreo cookies, scraped off the cream in the middle and replaced it with horseradish. He put Oreos in his lunch box. They were stolen the next day . . . and were never stolen again. I loved the "Oreo incident"! It was just so brilliant. Years later, that memory sparked the opening for my middle-grade novel *SLOB* in which the main character's Oreos are stolen from his lunchbox. Though the main character was initially based on my brother, he quickly developed his own personality, and the story took twists and turns that are far different from the real-life event. Use your memories to ignite story ideas, but then let your imagination take the lead.

- **Books, movies, TV shows.** Now obviously I'm not

suggesting you copy from your favorite book or movie. You can, however, borrow certain elements, like an unusual setting or a character's personality quirk or a specific conflict in the storyline. Remember, we're talking inspiration, not imitation!

- **Photos, Internet images, videos.** If you are more of a visual person, you can find loads of visual inspiration on the Internet. Set a timer so that you don't wind up spending hours in a deep dive. Scroll through images that interest you. It could be places, faces, supernatural beasts, whatever. If an image captures your imagination, print it out and tape it onto your wall near where you usually write, or keep it in a special inspiration notebook.

- **Nature.** It may feel like nothing much is happening in that cornfield or on that beach, but outer stillness makes room for things to happen inside your mind. Try it. Sit in a quiet part of a park or in the woods or by the ocean. Just be still. The ideas will sneak out of their hiding places and settle into your quiet mind.

- **News.** There used to be this old TV series called *Naked City*. It was a police drama, and at the end of each episode the narrator always said, "There are eight million stories in the naked city. This has been one of them." If you check out any city newspaper or any news site, you will find eight million stories. No, just kidding. Not eight million. But a lot.

- **Obituaries.** Okay, I know this is grim but, seriously, try it. Read some obituaries. I especially love reading the obituaries from the *New York Times* because the people who make it into that obit section have lived pretty interesting lives. I've read an obituary about a self-appointed prince of an island and an obituary about a guy who travelled across the country with his thirty goats. Real life *is* stranger than fiction.

- **Music.** Nothing creates a mood like music. Make your own playlist, close your eyes and let the music summon images in your mind.

- **Dreams.** Keep a notebook by your bed. You know how tricky dreams are. They slip away seconds after you open your eyes. If you have a good one, write it down as soon as you wake up.

- **Writing exercises.** When you are totally stumped

for a story idea, remind yourself that you write because it's fun. So have fun! Pick a writing exercise (there are a bunch in the #DIYWritingWorkshop section) and just play. Some of my best story ideas came from just messing around.

THREE

#TooManyIdeas!

While some writers struggle to come up with a single story idea, others have the opposite problem. For them, story ideas just won't leave them alone. No sooner do they start working on one story than another, "better" story idea taps them on the shoulder. They abandon the first story and tuck into the new one. But wait . . . once they have finished the first page, another "even better" idea is flagging them down, and they move on to that one.

The thing about new story ideas is that they are supercharged with excitement and potential . . . as long as they only stay in your head. Once you start writing them down, things change. You will probably run into trouble at some point. The words might stop flowing. Or maybe the characters seem to flatten out and become boring. That's why the next, newer idea is always so much more enticing.

Too many ideas often leads to a whole bunch of unfinished stories.

Swamp Mud

For a beginning writer, it's much more important to finish a story than to find the perfect story idea. The next time you start a story, keep going until it's done, even if you want to tear your hair out by the time you reach page five.

Just. Finish. It.

When you do, you will have had the experience of really wrestling with a story instead of just hopping from one to another. You will see what it feels like to drag yourself through the gross, swampy parts of your story and come out on the other side. You will understand the power of revision since, once you've finished a story, you can go back and polish up the chapters that were splattered with all that swamp mud. You will be doing the deep work that professional writers know must be done in order to create a good story.

#Writers911

#Stuckbusters

- New ideas are like frogspawn in that they start out blobby. They're interesting but unformed. They need time to grow legs and to look . . . froggy. Likewise, ideas need time to form and shape themselves. If you have a great story idea, wait a while before you start writing. Let it grow legs.

- When you get a stunningly brilliant idea while you are in the middle of writing another story, simply jot down the idea. Of course, you can use a journal, but I like to jot my ideas down on a piece of paper and put them it a special box on my writing desk. I use a Lego box that my son made for me, but you can use just about any container you like. I find having my story ideas literally within arm's reach is more reassuring than having them in a journal where they may be buried by other entries. I know that any time I feel like it, I can simply pluck a brilliant idea out of the box.

- If a new idea occurs to you while you are working on another story, consider if that new idea might work as a subplot in the current story. Don't force it, though. Just playfully see if it will fit in naturally.

- If you have several ideas and don't know which one to write first, talk to a trusted friend. I find that if I tell a friend about a bunch of story ideas, my voice will change when I'm talking about the idea that intrigues me the most (and luckily, even when I don't hear the change in my voice, my friends do and point it out). While some story ideas are really clever, it's the ideas that move us emotionally that are worth pursuing.

FOUR

#NoTimeToWrite
_____

Okay, strap on your crash helmet. We are going to talk about the sport of Extreme Writing. This is not for the faint of heart or the sloth-like. Extreme Writing is all about pouncing on those scraps of free-floating time in your life—yes, they are there, I promise—and seizing them in order to write.

We know that everybody is busy these days. Well, maybe not that guy who is always at the gym doing squats, but yeah, pretty much everyone else is busy. Some of us, though, are so insanely busy that writing seems like an impossibility. That's where Extreme Writing comes in. Many writers have squished writing into busy lives, myself included. We find those little writing opportunities in the day, even if they are only five- or ten-minutes long.

Extreme Writing may feel daunting at first. Your brain will feel flabby. Exhaustion plus flab will produce writing like this:

She opened the envelope and . . . it was a large envelope . . . the envelope was as full as a . . . she opened the very large envelope . . .

Yikes, right? But who cares? Even that dude at the gym can tell you that flab happens. But if you are relentless about seizing little writing opportunities throughout the day, you'll see things begin to firm up. You'll also discover that the more you write, the more time you'll find to write, and the more excited you'll be to write. And the beauty part is, your busy life will start to feed your writing life.

Extreme Writing

When I was waiting tables, I worked with former Tibetan monks, Cambodian refugees, an aspiring stand-up comedian, an amateur psychic, and many, many other interesting people. In fact, I think all writers should do a stint of waiting tables. Between your co-workers and your customers, you'll gather enough writing material to last for years.

Anyway, whenever I heard someone say or do something interesting in the restaurant, I would duck into the bathroom and scribble it down on an empty guest check. That took sixty seconds or less. Or when a diner was hemming and hawing about what they wanted, I'd smile and say, "Take your time." Then I'd flip to a blank guest check and jot down a sentence or two while they decided on their soup. It seems like nothing, but trust me, a sentence here . . . a line of dialogue there . . . it all added up. And perhaps more importantly, it kept my writing brain limber.

Since a big part of writing is thinking, one trick of Extreme Writing is to keep a piece of your mind on your story while you are doing other things. I don't mean that you always have to think about your writing; you'll certainly have times during the day when you need to put all your focus on school or a job. But there are also plenty of other times where you can do some mental multi-tasking. Let your mind play around with your story while you're doing menial tasks. When I was waiting tables, I'd imagine what sort of customers my characters might be. Would they be high-maintenance? Great tippers? Which waitress or waiter would they flirt with? Really, a healthy dose of story-obsession is not a bad thing. It will keep you submerged in your fictional universe, so that when those precious spare minutes appear, you'll be ready to use them.

Incidentally, keep some writing tools on hand! Nothing fancy. All you need is little notepad and a pen that you can tuck into your back pocket or in your bag. Or you might want to use a note-taking app, or dictate a few ideas into your phone. In a pinch, anything will do—a store receipt, a paper bag, toilet paper, the back of your hand. And just think what a great anecdote it will make when your story is finished, as in, "Yeah, I wrote this entire story on a roll of Charmin Ultra-Soft."

#Timebusters

Here are some suggestions for grabbing free-floating writing times:

- On a bus or train (and while waiting for one.)
- Waiting for an appointment.
- Getting up 15 minutes earlier than usual.
- While waiting for someone who is late (you'll never be angry at your chronically late friends again!)
- During boring meetings or lectures (be sly, though. I once got caught doing this at a job, and my boss told me he wasn't paying me good money so that I could write the Great American Novel).
- While babysitting (after the kids go to bed, of course.)
- Instead of watching TV or playing video games.
- At a restaurant, waiting for food to be served (thank you, slow-motion waitress, for the extra writing time).
- While being supportive and watching your friend play in a dead-boring game of soccer (just remember to cheer at the right moments).
- In the bathroom.
- Right before going to sleep.

FIVE

#MyIdeasStink!

Ideas are meant to get you amped up and eager to start scribbling. They're the triple espresso of the writing world. Sometimes, though, right after that initial adrenaline rush, you start to worry . . .

"Maybe the story isn't interesting enough."

"I think it's been done before."

"Is it too complicated?"

If you have an idea that excites you, don't start picking the poor thing to bits. Give it a chance. Begin writing and see where it takes you. Listen, there's a reason why cartoon characters have light bulbs over their heads when they get an idea, rather than a GPS. Ideas light up your brain but they aren't going to bark directions at you. Part of your job as a writer is to wander around with your lit-up brain and see what's in the neighborhood.

I often start out with one idea that leads me to another, and then another. By the end, there might be only a whiff of the original idea left in my story.

A few years ago, I decided to write about three siblings who were suffering from a tragic generational curse. As soon as I began writing, the kids burst out of my mind, almost fully formed. The setting was right, too. But the story line? *Hmm.* The more I wrote, the more I realized that the idea wouldn't work. Still, following that faulty storyline had led me to create these wonderful kids and to put them in just the right setting. In the end, my novel *The Kneebone Boy* became a completely different book than the one I had started to write. If I had totally trashed my original idea, I would never have arrived at the idea that worked.

The Stink Factor

On the other hand, can an idea just plain stink? Well, yes and no. It's not often that the idea itself stinks; it's just that it stinks for you, personally. Let's say you want to write about a poor but ambitious young woman in Victorian London who becomes a talented jewelry thief. Not a bad idea, right? But if you aren't tickled at the thought of doing lots of historical research, this idea might not work for you. You may love reading a certain genre, but writing it may not suit your temperament. Still, by all means, try it out. Write a few chapters and see if you secretly harbor a love for researching details of life in the19th century. Or maybe you prefer constructing a subterranean community of mutant lizards instead.

In many cases, though, the stink factor is subtler. Like so many things in writing, you can get a heads-up that an idea stinks (for you) through a gut feeling. Personally, I get this squirmy, uncomfortable sensation as I'm writing. But before abandoning my idea, I'll always try to push through it first. That's important. You may simply have hit a tough spot in your story, and if you just keep going, you'll find your way again.

Heads up, if you find yourself habitually starting with an idea, then deciding it's awful, moving on to another one and deciding that one is even worse, the problem may not be your ideas at all. It may be that you are simply getting stuck in the middle. (And guess what? I have a whole section called "Stuck in the Middle"! Just keep reading.) Sometimes, however, you may have an idea that really doesn't work. Here are a few ways to figure out if you have a "live one" or a stinker.

#Stinkbusters, er, Stuckbusters

Your idea might be a keeper if:

- It follows you around like a cocker spaniel, even if you tell it to go away.

- The idea still holds your interest after you've written a few pages. You can plunge right into the juiciest scene if you like. It doesn't matter if it lands you in the middle of the book or at the end. Now write another juicy scene. Just keep going without worrying about how the scenes are connected. You'll assemble the pieces later. Is your interest in the idea building with each scene? Good! That may mean you have a solid idea.

- Things are getting spooky. Do you suddenly notice echoes of your idea on the news, in overheard conversations, in an email from your friend? Don't dismiss these coincidences. They're little thumbs up from the universe to let you know you're going in the right direction.

SIX

#CreatingGreatCharacters

While in college, I met a girl named Kate who used to tell me about her friends back home. They were a strange and glamorous bunch, full of eccentric quirks and clever comebacks. Kate described them all so vividly that I soon felt like I knew them. They were special, cool, a little wild. She would tell me stories about their adventures and I would hang on her every word. I wanted to know everything they did, all the trouble they caused or got into, all their woes and dramas.

After we graduated, Kate and I remained friends. Bit by bit, I began to meet the friends she had told me about.

Guess what? They were all perfectly ordinary. Nice, for

sure, but nothing like the fabulous people whom Kate had described. Kate hadn't been lying about them. She just saw things in them that other people didn't.

Although Kate was not a writer, she understood the secret of great storytelling: If *you* find your characters interesting, other people will too. That seems obvious, but sometimes writers can have such a blindingly brilliant story idea that their characters become an afterthought. It's their story that captivates them, not their characters. No matter how great your story idea is, though, if you're not invested in your characters, your readers won't be invested in your story.

#Stuckbusters

- You can create your character from scratch or loosely base them on someone you know. Basing your character on someone you know can help you to imagine them clearly right from the beginning. A word of warning, though . . . borrow only one or two qualities from the real person to use for your character—like the freckles on their arms or their fear of balloons or the way they treat their little brother. You want to do this for two reasons. First, you don't want to offend anyone. Also, if your character is too much like the person you know, it will be hard to imagine them riding on the back of a giant blue lobster or fighting weapons smugglers or doing whatever else you may want them to do.

- You can also base your character on yourself, but again, you'll want to make them different from you. After all, this is fiction, right? If your character is based too closely on yourself, it will get in the way of your imagination.

- Before you even begin writing, have a nice, long chat with your characters. Get out your computer or a notebook and pencil and ask your character questions. Write down what you imagine their answers would be. Obviously, you can ask them any questions you like, but below are a few suggestions:

What kind of shoes are you wearing?

What does your bedroom look like?

What's your favorite thing about yourself, physically speaking (i.e. color of eyes, the fact that you are fast, double-jointed, hair, smile, etc.)?

What's your least favorite thing about yourself, physically?

What's the best part of your personality?

What's your biggest character flaw?

What scares you?

What are some things you are obsessed with?

Tell me about your family.

When you fight with your parents/friends, what is the argument most often about?

Tell me about your friends.

If your friends had to describe you, what would they say?

Do you have a secret?

Okay. Now we get to the most important question that you can ask your character. Ready? Here it is:

What do you want more than anything else?

Your character has to want something really badly. This is crucial. Maybe they want to be cast as the lead in the school play. Or maybe they want to find a secret underground tunnel that leads to their kidnapped brother. Or maybe they want a friend. It doesn't matter what they want, they just have to want it with all their heart.

Once you figure out what your character wants more than

anything else, you have to do something cruel. You have to make it really difficult for them to get it.

Like, *really* difficult.

That's how you pull your readers into your story and get them to root for your character. The stakes have to be high and the journey has to be difficult.

SEVEN

#FantasyWorldBuilding

Two of my friends once decided to build their own cabin. They had never built a cabin before. Let me just say that they are not the "plan ahead" types. They are the "let's wing it" types. Five months after they had finished building the cabin, a chunk of the ceiling fell down on their cat and gave it a concussion (who knew cats could even get concussions!).

Likewise, if you don't plan out your fictional world before you start your fantasy or dystopian story, that world might be too flimsy and, yes, collapse on your characters' heads.

#**S**tuckbusters

- Usually I'm not a fan of lots of pre-planning when it comes to stories. In my opinion pre-planning sucks all the fun out of writing. World building, however, does require some planning. There are lots of bits and pieces that you need to think about in order for a world to be functional. It might be a good idea to mull over some of these questions before you launch into your story . . .

What's the weather like in this world?

Is it a city or country landscape? Desert or woodsy or coastal or something completely new?

What do the animals and plants look like?

Who inhabits this world? Humans? Some other sort of creature?

Are there different ethnicities or religions? Different languages?

Is there a shortage of some resource, like food, water, or fuel? This is one way to immediately build conflict into your world.

Who has the power in your world? A king, a president, a wizard, a Wendigo (look it up!).

Do the inhabitants have jobs? Do they farm or hunt?

What is family life like in your world? How are children treated?

What do the inhabitants of this place value highly? A resource? A religion? A relic?

Do they have technology? If so, what kind?
   Do they have weapons?

What is your world's history? Recent wars? Famine?

Are there any old legends that affect the events in your story?

Is there any magic in your world? Magic works best when it comes with some rock-solid rules. How does the magic work? Spells, magical objects, potions, something else?

How do your characters gain the ability to use magic? Is it inborn? Do they learn it in a school or from a mentor? Are there some people who are naturally better at performing magic than others?

It's a good idea to put limitations on the magic. If your character can always use magic to get out of any problem, nothing is at stake and that's no fun. Are there situations when the magic won't work or will backfire spectacularly?

What is the magic used for? Are there several types of magic that are used for different purposes?

Is there a price to pay for doing magic? For instance, do people have to leave home for years to study it? Does using magic affect your mind or body or soul?

Are there any magical means of transportation?

- If building a fantasy world from scratch makes you nervous, try world blending. That's when you take pieces of the world that you know and merge them with elements of a fantasy world. Blending worlds gives you the advantage of working within a familiar setting. You don't have to make up all the rules, just a few of them. And the mix of the familiar with the bizarre can be powerful and even funny. For instance, maybe the school in your story is exactly like your school except that the teachers are all ghosts of famous historical figures like King Tut and Amelia Earhart. Or maybe the local library looks and operates exactly like your local library, except that instead of lending books, they lend superhuman abilities.

- Remember, your story is always, always, ALWAYS about your characters first and foremost. Your characters can cast the most spectacular spells in the spell book, but if their personalities are meh, the story will be meh too.

EIGHT

#Who'sTellingTheStory?

We've all experienced this. Two of your friends tell you about the same event—like a party or an argument—and each person brings a totally different spin to the story. Maybe your friend with the dry sense of humor makes the event sound ridiculous; and maybe your other, more serious friend makes it sound tragic. Point-of-view (POV) can make all the difference.

Sometimes you know who should be telling the story the moment you start writing. It just feels right. The voice spills out naturally and easily.

Other times, though, it's not at all clear who should tell

the story. Sure, your main character with the wise-cracking attitude could narrate it. That would be entertaining. But if her brilliant and sensitive best friend narrated it instead, he would bring some depth to the story. Then again, you could "head hop" between the two of them, seeing things from both their perspectives. *Gaaah,* choices!

When you are stumped as to which POV you should use, you need to test drive them. Write a few chapters from different perspectives. Yes, it takes some extra time, and yes, you will have to scrap some of those chapters but hey, you wouldn't buy a car without seeing how it handles on the highway, right?

Okay, let's have a look at the pros and cons of different point of view (POV for short):

First person POV

For some reason, I think of first-person narrative in terms of smell. You know when someone sits so close to you that you can smell their breath or their shampoo or the laundry detergent on their clothes? Or maybe the clothes haven't been through the wash cycle for a while and smell sour? Well, when you write in the first person, your readers sits right next to the narrator and can smell them, full-strength, throughout the whole story. Let's see how this works using a character named Lester as our first-person narrator . . .

> I didn't want the tattoo in the first place. For one thing, I'm the biggest coward you've ever met. Seriously. I once passed out during an eye exam. It was Jenny who talked me into getting the tattoo because that girl can talk me into anything.
> The moment the tattoo artist walked in, I knew I was going to regret this. The guy was a freak. He had a long black ponytail and his eyes were lined with black eyeliner and he wore a silver-sequined T-shirt. I felt a single cool droplet of sweat leak down the back of my neck and dribble between my shoulder blades. Jenny smashed it by slapping me on my back.
> "He's ready," she told the guy.

First-person POV is intensely personal, which can make it fascinating to write, and to read. No other POV pulls you into the story so immediately. It's raw. You are eavesdropping on someone's very soul. The first-person narrator's voice needs to be authentic and interesting, though, so that your reader will actually want to eavesdrop on their soul.

Third-person Limited POV

With this perspective, there's a distance between the storyteller and the story. The narrator will guide you into the heart and mind of one particular character, but the narration won't feel quite as cozy as the first-person POV. The narrator can tell readers what the character's breath smells like, but your readers won't feel like they are smelling it up close and personal.

The advantage of this POV is that you see the story through the eyes of one character. Your reader will get to know that character's thoughts, motives, and emotions, while the other characters' motives can remain a bit mysterious. This leaves room for misunderstandings or uncertainty, and that, of course, can lead to conflict and we all love conflict—at least the fictional kind.

Okay, here is our third-person limited narrator who is focused on Lester . . .

Lester's eyes widened as the tattoo artist snapped on a pair of black latex gloves and then picked up his tattoo gun.

"Aren't you supposed to sketch the design on my arm first?" Lester asked. Nerves had made his voice sound strangely high.

"That's not how this works," the tattoo artist said flatly. He switched on the gun and a loud buzzing sound filled the room.

Lester felt the sharp sting of the gun as it hummed across the skin on his right forearm. Jenny grabbed his left hand and held it tightly. Her hand felt small and cool and reassuring. Grateful, Lester looked over at her. To his bewilderment, he found that Jenny's green eyes were fixed on the tattoo gun, her expression filled anticipation. Anticipation for what, though, he couldn't begin to imagine.

Third-Person Omniscient POV

Omniscient POV is the "security guard" of POVs. I imagine the omniscient narrator sitting in a black swivel chair, surrounded by monitors that show all the characters going about their business. The security guard can tell readers what each character is doing and thinking and feeling.

Obviously, the main advantage of this POV is that your narrator's focus can jump around between characters, which can add different layers to the story.

Another advantage is that your narrator can have their own unique way of looking at this fictional world. If the narrator has a sarcastic sense of humor, all the drama swirling around the characters might look pretty humorous. Or the narrator could be far wiser than any of the characters, giving the reader deep insight into the characters' actions.

Let's peek in on Lester again, this time with third-person omniscient...

Poor Lester. Yet again he had done something to impress Jenny, and yet again she didn't seem to notice. She only had eyes for the tattoo itself. She watched, fascinated, as the blue ink begin to take form across Lester's forearm. It was not a phoenix, as Lester had requested. It wasn't a bird at all. Instead, the tattoo artist was inking a word into Lester's skin.

"Wait! You're making a mistake!" Lester cried and tried to pull his arm away, but the tattoo artist clamped his hand down Lester's wrist.

"No mistake, mate," the tattoo artist said. "Keep still or it will hurt more."

"It will be okay, Lester," Jenny told him, feeling a stab of guilt at the lie.

The tattoo artist held the tattoo gun loosely while it made its slow way across the boy's skin, moving on its own. The tattoo artist simply kept it steady and watched with interest as the word formed. HAPEX. It was the code that would keep this kid alive in the coming weeks, if he was lucky. And this kid, the tattoo artist thought grimly as he looked at the boy's ashen face, did not look lucky.

The Second-Person POV

This one is weird. Not many writers use it. However, if you do it well it can be pretty interesting. In this POV, the reader ("you") is the character.

What this POV does is make the reader part of the story, so that they are instantly immersed. Here goes . . .

You watch the letters form. HAPEX. What does it mean? you wonder. Why would that psycho tattoo dude write it on your arm? You groan. Why did you do this in the first place, you think. Your mom is going to kill you. And your dad? Forget about it. You look at Jenny and her eyes meet yours. Then she leans over and rolls down her sock so you can see what's on her ankle. It's a tattoo. It also says HAPEX.

#*S*tuckbusters

- Write a diary installment in the voice of your first-person narrator. It can be about some incident that happens in the story, their thoughts on another character in the story, a play-by-play of a day in their life, or something else. This is a good way to hear the character's voice and help determine whether or not it can carry the story.

- Write a scene from the POV of a very minor character. Sometimes there is a character lurking in your story that has a compelling narrative voice.

- Here's a writing prompt that will help you explore the Third-Person Omniscient POV:

Four people are trapped in an elevator that is stuck between floors. Use the third-person omniscient POV to write the scene, head-hopping between your different characters. You can explore what each character is feeling about the situation, what they think of each other, and how their thoughts and feelings might change as the clock ticks on.

- Here's a writing prompt that will help you explore first-person and third-person limited POVs:

A detective is investigating someone's disappearance. Write the scene in which the detective discovers the missing person from:

1. The third-person limited POV, in which the narrator is focused on the detective.
2. The first-person POV in which the narrator is the missing person.

NINE

#Research

If I had to list my favorite things about writing, doing research would be in the top ten, right next to "The ability to work in my pajamas." In fact, I think research is downright healthy for writers. It stretches your mind, your legs, and often your comfort zones. While doing research I have visited a county jail cell, ridden on a speeding mail boat, learned skateboarding tricks from a teenage pro, and interviewed a NYC subway conductor.

These days, I often choose certain storylines precisely

because I know nothing about them. For me, half the fun of writing is learning something I didn't know before.

There are several ways that a writer can gather information: the Internet; books and periodicals; personal experience; and interviewing experts. I like to start with the most accessible information—usually the Internet—and gradually expand my sources of information.

Online Deep Dive

In both research and writing, you have to dive deep in order to find the really good stuff. Sure, you can find plenty of online facts about any given subject, but facts alone won't create magic—and by magic I mean the ability to breathe life into your characters and your story. For that, you need to work a little harder.

Let's say that you want to write about an Olympic gymnast. And let's say that you're not an Olympic gymnast. Let's also say that you don't happen to know any Olympic gymnasts (although you may . . . see Go Pro). It's easy enough to Google things like "How many hours do Olympic gymnasts train every week?" (About 30 hours in the gym, give or take). It's tempting to just insert a lot of facts into your story to make your gymnast's life believable, but your gymnast is more than just a collection of facts. She is a real kid—or she will be once you've worked your magic.

One of the keys to using research wisely is to find the small but crucial details. Sometimes learning the general facts will lead you to those small details. For instance, now that you've learned that your gymnast spends 30 hours a week in the gym, let your imagination play with this information. *Hmm*, what do those gyms look like? Maybe you can watch some videos of Olympic gymnasts training in their gyms. Put the video's speed setting on slow so that you catch all the details, like the height of the walls or the cubbies for water bottles. Are there any signs with inspirational quotes? And wait, if you have a bunch of people training in the gym thirty hours a week, what the heck does the place smell like?! If you Google that question, you'll discover that the balance beam smells of sweaty feet and chalk . . . now that's an interesting little detail that will strike a chord of authenticity in your story. And if you Google "interviews with gymnasts," you might discover that for a gymnast, everything looks like gym equipment—a stretch of field is begging for a tumbling pass; a stone wall is perfect for a split leap. Details like these are treasures that will give your gymnast a pulse and make your readers see her world—and smell those sweaty feet.

Virtual Globetrotting

If you are writing about an actual place that you don't know well—or at all—the very best thing you can do is go there. Of course, that's not always possible, but don't worry . . . there are several ways to get there without actually getting there.

The quickest way to explore a place is to use Google Street Maps. You can travel down the luxurious streets of Dubai or the suburban sprawl of Levittown, New York. It will give you a general feel for a place—the buildings, the stores, the cars people drive. Is it cheating? Sure. There is obviously no replacement for the real thing, but not all of us can jet over to London to research a scene set on the River Thames. Google Street Map and a generous helping of your imagination may be enough to build a convincing scene that is set in a place you've never been. The biggest problem with Google Maps is you might find yourself "wandering around" Paris for the afternoon instead of writing.

Of course, if you know someone who lives or has lived in the place, ask them if they would mind chatting with you about their experience and show you some photos (see Interviewing Tips). You can also read travel memoirs and guides, as well as novels that are set in the location you are writing about. You might check out some movies or TV shows that are set in the place you are studying, or watch some YouTube travel videos. One of my personal favorite ways to get the flavor, literally, of a place is to watch TV shows that explore its cuisine. It's amazing how much you can learn about a place's culture by studying its food.

Leg Work

Remember, if you only stick to Internet and book research, you'll be missing out on a much richer vein of knowledge. Step away from your computer. Do some legwork. If you are writing about a certain location, visit it if possible. Google Street Maps, while hugely helpful, can't compete with seeing a place in person—touching the marble toes of a statue; smelling the sweet, musty air of an old farm; hearing the sound of a buoy-bell ringing with the ocean's swells. These are the little details that will give your work a much more layered and authentic feel than simply weaving in facts from a website.

A few years ago, I wrote the *Piper Green* series, about a little girl who lives on an island in Maine. Her father is a lobsterman, and in one of the books Piper helps her father on his lobster boat. Having never gone lobster fishing myself, I did all sorts of research online. Was it helpful? Definitely. Still, I knew that, if possible, I should experience lobster fishing firsthand. I asked around (read about the Six Degrees of Separation theory in Go Pro) and wound up with several invitations to go lobster fishing. Since my character would be helping out on the boat, I asked them to put me to work. I was given the job of stuffing the bait bags with dead herring. If I had simply stuck to my Internet research, I might never have discovered how oily your hands feel when you handle bait fish. Or that the smell of dead fish lingers on your clothes through three washings. Or how lobster traps catch all sorts of things besides lobster—crabs and starfish and eels—so that each haul is like opening a treasure chest. When I wrote the lobster fishing scene in *Piper Green*, I was able to incorporate these details in the hopes that my readers would fully experience Piper's day on the boat . . .without having to wash their clothes three times over.

Go Pro

A great way to gather information about something is to speak to an expert on the subject. An expert can tell you things you won't be able to glean from the Internet or books.

I often find my experts through people I know. Over the years, I've interviewed a professional skateboarder, a New York City subway conductor, a sheriff, and a secret service agent for a U.S. President. They were all people I either knew directly or was introduced to by a friend, or a friend of a friend of a friend.

"You must know some very interesting people." That's what you're thinking, right? Well, I do. And so do you, although you may not realize it. There's this thing called Six Degrees of Separation. Maybe you've heard of it. It's the theory that everybody on earth is only six introductions away from anyone else. So although you may not personally know an Olympic gymnast, you might know someone who is related to someone who is best friends with another person whose cousin is dating someone whose younger sister is an

Olympic gymnast. Got it? In other words, if you are looking for an expert, ask around. There may just be a chain of connections that will put an expert within your reach.

Understandably, some writers feel shy about approaching experts whom they don't know. They think, "Why would this person waste their time talking to me?" Remember, people love to talk about the things they know best. Chances are, if you call that reptile specialist at the zoo, she'll talk your ear off about Flying Geckos.

When I was working on a novel and needed to write a scene set in a jail cell, I approached the local sheriff for some advice. He gave me a detailed tour of the cells. In fact, he was so happy to chat about the facilities that by the end of our tour I even knew how to escape a jail cell (my lips are sealed).

When the Six Degrees of Separation theory fails and I can't track down an expert personally, there is always YouTube. In a pinch, videos of experts being interviewed can be quite helpful. Of course, you can read interviews of these folks too, but I think videos give you a better feel for the people—how they speak, how they dress, their facial expressions. I once had to write about a character that repaired antique pottery, so I watched a video interview of a man who did that for a living. Zzzz, right? But in the video the man described his profession as a dangerous dance on a high wire, where you were caught between revealing the original beauty of a piece of pottery and possibly ruining a priceless piece of history. His intensity, the way he spoke so softly as he worked, as though his voice alone could damage the vase, gave me a whole new perspective on my character.

Current Events

When you are researching online, remember to check dates to make sure the information is current. For instance, I had been looking for information on why worms always come out in wet weather. Haven't you ever wondered about that? When I looked it up on the Internet, I found many sites that said it was because they might drown in their water-filled burrows. But when I narrowed my search to the past year, I found that current research says something quite different. Scientists now believe that earthworms come out in the rain because it's easier for them to migrate over land when the soil is wet. (There. Now you can impress your friends with worm trivia.) Information is often changing at lightning speed, so make sure your research is as up-to-date as possible.

Historical Fiction

If you are writing historical fiction, you should probably decide on how specific you want to be right from the beginning. Will it be enough to research everyday life, such as clothing, furniture, and what people ate? Or do you want to get more specific and research the politics at that time, women's roles, the way the rich treated the poor? Do you need to know what the popular culture was? What sort of music was played or which dances were danced?

In order to immerse your readers in another time period,

you have to be immersed in it yourself. For historical research, archives are your best friend. Many museums, universities and libraries have archives available to the public —both online and in person. In these archives you might find photos, books, diaries, letters, and much more. It takes time and patience to dig through the vast amounts of material but it will be worth your while.

Of course, reading many non-fiction books about that time period, as well as fiction books set in that time period, is crucial. You should read books that were written *during* that time period too. Apart from reading old letters and diaries, there's no better way to get a sense of how people spoke, lived and thought back in the day.

If it's possible to visit historical sites where scenes in your story may have occurred, do it! Stepping on the soil where a battle was fought or where an orphanage once existed will feed your imagination. You can also visit museums to see artifacts of the time period (if possible, take a museum tour. Tour guides know all the best stories and can answer your questions).

There is one pitfall of writing historical research, however. You may become so immersed in your research that . . . well, go on and read the next section.

A Few Words of Warning

It's possible to be so immersed in your research that your story becomes an afterthought. Each time you discover a juicy new tidbit of information, you think, "Ooo, I'll include that!" Then you try to squish the information into your story, even if it doesn't really fit. Your story and your characters need to come first. Always.

Try not to get all show-offy with your newfound knowledge. Research should be woven into the story in the most natural way possible. Dumping a whole lot of facts into your story just to prove that you know what you're talking about is never a good idea.

Like this:

Julie revved her lightweight, off-road dirt bike with its stiff suspension. She was getting ready for the competition of Freestyle Motocross, also known as FMX. Today she'd be going for a front flip, which had been attempted by Jim Dechamp in 2008 resulting in him breaking his back.

---

*Y*eah, that's waaaaay too much information. The last thing you want is for your readers to think, "Wow, the author really did their research on motocross racing." On the contrary, you want your readers to forget all about you. Author? What author? The only thing they should be thinking about is Julie's motocross race against an undercover assassin . . . or whatever predicament you have cooked up for the poor girl.

When to Research

Should you research your story before you start writing your story? Or should you start writing your story and research what you need to know when you need it? Like so many things in writing, it's a personal preference. Some people like to gather as much knowledge as they can before they even write the first sentence of their story. Others like to gather information as they go along.

Personally, I like to do my research on a specific subject while I'm writing about that subject. For one thing, research can become an excellent excuse to procrastinate because, let's face it, it's easier to research than to actually buckle down and write. Also, my story may not be going in the direction I think it is. For instance, I may think my character is going to become a dolphin rehabilitator, but as the story unfolds, I see he's much more likely to build an orphanage in the mountains of Nepal. If I've done all my research ahead of time, I'm going to have wasted oodles of hours on researching dolphin behavior.

However, if you are a meticulous plotter and don't have a tendency to procrastinate, you may be better off doing your research before you launch into writing. That may give you a strong feel for the setting and situation before you begin. It also may help keep your story momentum on track since you won't have to stop and dive into research as often.

Organizing Research

Even a little bit of research can quickly turn into a disorganized mess. You may start drowning in dozens of bookmarked websites, scribbles on the back of envelopes, and chaotic piles of notebooks. If you don't organize your research, you may find yourself reading your notes and thinking "Wait! Why exactly did I want to know how to milk a water buffalo?"

There are several good ways to go about organizing your research, ranging from the super simple to the high tech. Again, whatever works best for you is the best method.

You can use a loose-leaf notebook with tabs to organize your research. It can be separated by character, topic, time frame, or scenes. If it's historical, you can separate it by clothes, lifestyle, vernacular, politics, etc. Index cards work as well. If you like a more in-your-face, visual approach, a cork board can be helpful.

There are also some good software programs that will help you organize your research. I've used Scrivener and found it useful, but there are lots of others (and no doubt more on the way). If you are more visual, there are apps and software that create "maps" for your research, connecting information by lines and shapes.

Again, experiment with different strategies and see which ones speak to you.

 Stuckbusters

Here are some tips that can help you conduct a great interview with an expert:

- When you contact your interviewee, explain exactly what information you are looking for and how much of their time you'll need to complete the interview. *(Of course, if you are a kid, always check with your parents first before contacting anyone!)

- Be prepared. Have a list of questions ready. Also, it might be helpful to present them with a scenario that you will be using in your book: "Okay, my character falls onto the subway tracks just as the R train is pulling into the station. What would have to happen in order for her to escape with minor injuries?"

- Record your interview (of course, first check if the person you are interviewing is okay with being recorded). It's easy to get so caught up in the conversation that you forget to jot things down.

- Don't be too uptight about sticking to your pre-planned questions. It's often when the expert goes "off-topic" that you'll hear the most interesting stuff.

- You can ask your interviewee to take you through a typical day. That leaves room for all kinds of side stories and it allows the interviewee to sink into the subject naturally.

- If you said that the interview would take an hour, be true to your word. If your interviewee offers to give you a little more time, great!

- Transcribe your notes or your recording ASAP, when the details are fresh in your mind.

- At the end of the interview, you can ask your interviewee if it would be okay to contact them with any follow-up questions. Also, if there were questions that they weren't able to answer, perhaps they can refer you to other experts in the field.

- After your interview, be sure to send an e-mail or note in the mail thanking them for their time.

TEN

#ShouldIWrite2Stories@Once?

The question is not so much *should* you but *can* you write two stories at once? For some writers, juggling two or more stories simultaneously works quite well. Neil Gaiman, for example, says that he will write two or three books at the same time. When he is feeling blocked on one book, he'll just switch to writing another one. If that works for you, too, consider yourself very fortunate. Not only does that give you a strategy to deal with writer's block, it will also make you very prolific!

Personally, I find that writing two books simultaneously works best if the books are very different. For instance, while writing this book, I am also writing a middle-grade novel. The two books have virtually nothing in common. When I get stuck writing one of these books, I put it aside and tuck into the other book. This way I can keep the creativity flowing.

I have tried writing two fiction books at the same time, and frankly I found it difficult. It reminds me of attempting to learn French and Spanish simultaneously. At some point you are going to mix them up and say something silly like, *"El nino va a chez moi."* The main character from one of my novels started to sound an awful lot like the main character from the other novel. My first-person narration in one book started seeping into the other book, which was told in third person. My brain just couldn't handle two fiction stories at once.

I don't have any Stuckbusters for you here, except to try it and see what works for you.

ELEVEN

#NamingCharacters

There's this great fantasy series called *The Earthsea Trilogy* by Ursula K. Le Guin. In the series, everyone has a "True Name," which is different from the name that people call them. In order for magicians to work magic on someone or some thing, they must know its True Name.

I always think about that book when I am trying to name my characters. It does seem like every character has a True Name. If you can find it, you can work your own brand of magic by bringing that character to life.

How do you know what your character's True Name is? Usually I know it when I hear it. When I say the name out loud, I might see my character in front of me. Maybe I'll even notice a few things I hadn't noticed before—a small birthmark on the side of their chin, a chipped tooth, or the way they pick at the cuticle on their thumb when they're worried. Sometimes though, it's more subtle than that. There's just a certain *rightness* to the name. It fits the character like a favorite T-shirt and you just can't imagine them being called anything else.

#Stuckbusters

- Think about your character's parents. After all, they would have been the ones to name your character, right? Consider the parents' heritage. Are they Latino, Jewish, African- American, Japanese? Are they earthy people who might name a child something like River or Dragonfly? Or are they more conventional (John, Emily and Daniel)?

- Maybe your character's parents noticed something special about their baby and named them accordingly. The baby who smiled all the time might have been named Blythe. Or the infant whose legs never stopped moving might have been named Dash.

- Consider the year your character was born. If your character's parents were the conventional types, you can look up the most popular baby names of that year.

- Baby name web sites and books offer oodles of possibilities, with the added advantage of often having the names' meanings attached. Knowing the meaning of your character's name can add a layer of depth to your character. For instance, if your character is a girl who is the only voice of reason in a chaotic family, a name like Laney (torch of light) might be fitting. Or if your character is a Minotaur prince who rescues a human baby from baby-eating Death Worms, a name like Prince Rakim (to show mercy) might work.

- When you are writing fantasy fiction, naming things get a little more complicated. If your names are exotic, make sure that readers can pronounce them. A name like Yastrezhemsky won't exactly roll off the tongue. The names also have to fit the fantasy world you've created. Is it a primitive world or highly evolved? Are there tribes with distinct sounding names? Do wealthy people have different sorts of names than the poor?

- You can take familiar names and tweak them for a more unusual sound (Francine might become Francille or Steven might become Stivan). And as many of you already know, there are loads of fantasy name generators that will spit out names for anything from Orcs to dragons.

- I like leafing through phone books for last names. Yes, phone books do still exist! I can kill the better part of an afternoon poring over names in the phone book, but it's often worth it. I've found some remarkable last names this way, like Rattlebags and Kneebone.

- You can borrow names from people you know, but be careful! Don't use the same first and last name. Also if you suspect that person will be offended if you use either name, don't do it. Just don't. It's not worth it.

- As you consider names, be conscious of the immediate impression they may make. What do you think Sebastian P. Vanderhoven looks like? How about Pip Bunn? Or Edna Trout?

- If you have collected a list of potential names, say them out loud. Do they flow or are they hard to say? Personally, I try to avoid hard-to-pronounce names because I always worry that my readers are saying the name wrong. (I did use a hard-to-pronounce name in my book *The Kneebone Boy*, but I actually tell the readers how to properly pronounce the name Lucia).

- Mix and match. Your larger-than-life character can have a perfectly bland name. I think it's a fun challenge to take a very ordinary name, like Jane for instance, or maybe something old mannish, like Hermon, and attached it to an extraordinary character. Your readers will never think of Janes and Hermans the same way again!

- Think twice about giving two characters names that sound similar or share first letters, such as Laura and Larissa, Alan and Adam, Mia and Nya. You'll wind up confusing your readers and make it hard for them to get a good grip on your characters.

- If you think you've hit on the True Name, give it a test drive. Write a few scenes in which your character goes by that name. If the name doesn't fit, you'll feel it. I often think I've hit on the perfect name, but when I start writing, I realize I was wrong. If that happens to you, don't let it stop you from writing. You can use a "working name" until you discover your character's True Name.

- Wake up in the morning and tell yourself you are going to find the name of your character today. Then go about your business but pay attention! The name might pop up in a weird way. You might hear someone yell it out on the street. Or you might hear it on TV or in a song. Things can get freaky when you write with intention.

TWELVE

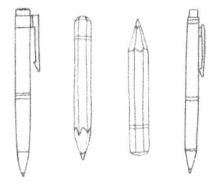

#TheAntihero

Does your main character have to be likable?
The simple answer is no. Your character is your creation, and they can be the most despicable person on the planet, if that's what you want.

The more complicated answer is . . . **yes**, your character does have to be likable. Because although your character is your creation, I'm assuming you also want people to read your story. It can be difficult for a reader to get behind a main character that is truly unlikable. Readers root for characters they admire or relate to or feel sympathy toward. If your main character is a vicious young emperor who tortures anyone who badmouths him, your readers are not going to care if he is captured by his enemy's troops and punished. In fact, they'll probably be glad.

But wait, the even more complicated answer is that you *can* have an unlikable main character as long as you can find something about them that truly is likable. It's not hard really. Think about someone you really dislike. Now try and remember one instance when they showed vulnerability. Maybe you saw their feelings get hurt by something someone said. Or maybe you saw them when they were sick or in pain. You can feel sympathy for even the most flawed person when you see them as defenseless or hurt. Likewise, if you can find the vulnerability in your main character, you can coax your readers to root for even the most diabolical villains.

#Stuckbusters

Below are a few steps to help readers feel warm and fuzzy about a not-so-nice nice character:

- Whenever I'm struggling to find some redeeming quality in a person whom I dislike, I imagine them as a little kid. Little kids are pretty transparent. They haven't yet learned to mask their heartbreak or their fears or insecurities. Personally, I find it hard to dislike little kids, even the really annoying ones. Try to imagine your character as child (if they already are a child, try to imagine them a bit younger). How did their parents treat them? Did they have siblings, and what was your character's relationship to them? Any friends? What made them cry? What were they most afraid of? In our emperor's case, maybe his parents barely noticed him when he was a child. Or maybe he witnessed his parents' assassination, and he was raised by adults who didn't much care for him. Maybe he has a fear of being assassinated, too, and rarely goes outside the palace. Connecting to a younger version of your hard-to-like character may help you to see a softer, more fragile side of them.

- Put your character in a difficult situation, emotionally or physically, or both. Make them struggle. Let's go back to our nasty young emperor who has been captured by the enemy. Maybe he's forced to work in the fields for hours each day, under the blazing sun. If he doesn't work hard enough, he's beaten. The other servants know about his privileged past and they hate him for it. Any chance they get, they will steal what little food he's given. He's hungry, tired, and bruised. If you do a good job describing his miserable life as a captive, your readers may begin feel a twinge of pity for him. That's when you move on to the next #Stuckbuster . . .

- Let your character have a change of heart. In the example of our emperor, he might befriend some of the other servants. Or maybe he even falls in love with one of them. Having experienced suffering firsthand, he can now feel empathy for people in a way he couldn't before. The evolution of a character from villain to hero is powerful and dramatic. In some ways, an unlikable character that grows into a likable one can be even more appealing than a character that starts off as a decent human being.

THIRTEEN

#ReadyToWriteANovel?

Do you know someone who is so lanky that they always look squished when they're sitting in a car? They are constantly fidgeting and jiggling and stretching their arms and legs in small spaces?

A lot of writers feel that way when they try to fit their ideas into a short story. They feel cramped. Their imaginations are BIG. They don't like to confine their stories to ten pages or so. It's a novel or nothing.

That's why you may not like what I have to say next.

Before you launch into writing a novel, it's a good idea to write (and finish) as many short stories as possible. I learned how to write novels by writing, and reading, short stories. In some ways, short stories were better teachers than many of the creative writing professors I had in college.

Here are some advantages to writing short stories:

- You can actually finish a short story. It typically takes me about a year to a year and a half to finish a novel. It took me ten years to finish my first novel!

A short story, on the other hand, can be finished in a matter of weeks, maybe days, depending on the writer. If you've tried to write a novel (or several novels) and never actually finished it, you haven't truly learned how to write a story. You haven't experienced moving through the arc of a story, letting your characters fully experience a storyline that challenges them and changes them forever. And you don't know what it's like to type THE END and mean it.

- Typically, short stories have far fewer characters than novels. For beginning writers, it's easier to focus on fully developing one or two characters than to juggle a dozen or more in a novel.

- A novel's plot might have many peaks and valleys while a short story generally has one peak. Concentrating on a simpler storyline helps you to focus on how to skillfully build tension and resolve it. For novice writers, juggling multiple story threads may be overwhelming. To be honest, it can be pretty overwhelming for professional writers too.

- Short stories often (though not always) deal with a more compressed time frame than a novel. Writing a story that occurs within the space of a few days or hours is a lot easier to handle than writing a novel that might span across years.

*O*f course, short story writing is much more than just a warm-up exercise for novelists. In some ways, writing a great short story is harder than writing a great novel. That's because when you write a short story, you have very few words to mess around with. It's the difference between being given $200 to spend on groceries for the week or given only $10. If you have only $10, you are going to want to get the most bang for your buck. You're probably not going to buy Pop Tarts and a jumbo pack of AAA batteries. You're going to buy the things that that will keep your belly full and your body functioning (at least I hope so!). When you are writing a short story, every word should either help build your character or advance the story's action.

#**S**tuckbuster

- Go the library and get your hands on a good anthology of short stories. There are oodles of them, with story collections ranging from the classics to more contemporary fiction. Leaf through them and see which ones catch your eye. There are also many classic short stories that you can read online for free. Some of my favorite short story writers are Flannery O'Connor, Truman Capote, J.D. Salinger, Alice Walker, Colette, Stephen King, and Nora Zeale Hurston.

- Read the short stories with a writer's eye. In fact, it's best if you read them twice—once just for the fun of it, and again to dissect it. Try and figure out why a character really grabbed you and pulled you into a story. Was it something they said or the way they behaved in a difficult situation? Was it the way the author described them physically? What part of the story was most interesting? How did the writer use words to get you to feel or think something? Where did the story peak? How about the ending . . . did it feel rushed or smooth; was it satisfying or did it leave you wondering what the heck happened? After you finished the story, did you find yourself thinking about a certain part of it, or one character in particular?

FOURTEEN

#PenOrComputer?

Should you write on a computer or by hand? Like so many other things in writing, there is no right or wrong here. If a great notebook and pen get you fired up, write by hand. If the words flow better when they travel from your brain into your keyboard, then by all means, write on your computer.

Personally, I write both ways at very specific times. I almost always write by hand when I first start a book. Just the act of picking up my pen and looking down at a blank piece of paper puts my brain on notice: "Okay, Brain, for the next hour we will be creating a new world together. Ready? Go!"

Once my book is flowing and I feel like I've got a strong footing in my fictional world, I switch to a computer for speed and efficiency. When I get stuck—and I always get stuck—I go back to writing by hand again until the flow returns.

But that's just me. You might have a totally different approach and that's fine too. Experiment and see what works best.

#*S*tuckbusters

Advantages of Writing by Hand

- Since most of us do our everyday writing (emails, note-taking) by computer, writing by hand sends an automatic signal to our brains that we will be doing a different kind of writing.

- I like the fact that if I write by hand, I can write anywhere, any time. If I'm in a restaurant and I get an idea for a line of dialogue or a description, I can whip out my notebook and jot it down. I can write comfortably at the beach or while waiting to get my hair cut or if I get a sudden idea while in the mall bathroom.

- Writing by hand is slower, and that can be a good

thing. In order to think deeply we need to slow down.

- For all you pen-and-notebook geeks like me, using cool notebooks and beautiful pens can be very inspiring.

- When you write by hand and then type it into the computer, you will naturally begin to edit. This extra bit of editing as you transcribe is always a plus.

- It helps deepen your focus, since writing by hand rather than a computer automatically cuts out a major source or distraction, namely the Internet and all those viral videos of dogs on trampolines.

Advantages of Writing on a Computer

- Obviously, it's a faster way to write since you don't have to transcribe from handwritten work.

- If your words flow faster than you can scribble by

hand, writing on a computer may feel more comfortable.

- Writing on a computer is a definitely a better option if your handwriting is hard to read.

- If you like to rearrange scenes as you're writing, and you feel like it's confusing to do it when writing by hand, a computer might be the better option.

FIFTEEN

#WritingPartners

Years ago, when I was about halfway through writing my first novel, I got stuck. Massively stuck. I did what most beginning writers do. I put the novel aside and promised myself I'd get back to it in a few days. I believed myself too. But after a few days, I still didn't feel ready yet, so I told myself I'd start at the beginning of the following week. Fast forward to one year later. Guess how much work I've done on that novel. Yup. None.

At the time I was waiting tables at a Thai restaurant. A new girl was hired. She was smart and edgy, with spiky hair, red-framed glasses and a nose ring. We started talking and it turned out that she was also in the middle of writing a novel. And she was also stuck. So we made a pact to email one page of writing to each other every single day, seven days a week until our novels were finished. We wrote out the details of the pact on a piece of paper, rolled it up, stuck it in a bottle and flung the bottle into a lake. It was quite dramatic. And it worked. Every day I wrote one page of my novel and emailed it to her. She did the same.

At first, our work was awful. If we hadn't made the pact, I probably would have stopped working on the novel altogether since nothing I wrote was even usable. Still, since I had made a promise to her, I kept sending her my daily page. And you know what? After a few weeks, my writing started to get better. So did hers.

When we were working at the restaurant, rolling up silverware in cloth napkins or filling sauce bottles, we talked about our characters and what they might do next. We discussed their relationships and their stints in jail and their weird scientific experiments in the hidden grotto beneath their house. Our co-workers thought we were talking about real (and very weird!) people because that's how our characters felt to us.

Then came a day when I just didn't feel like writing my page. So I didn't. I figured my writing partner wouldn't even notice. Or if she noticed, she'd understand. Around 11:30 at night there was a knock on my door. It was my writing partner demanding my page. She sat down and waited for me to write it. After that I never missed a day, and neither did she.

Roughly six months after we made our pact we both

finished our novels within days of each other. After I revised it, I submitted it to a literary agent and months later a publisher bought it.

I truly believe that the only reason I was able to finish that first novel was because I had found a good writing partner.

If you have a friend who also loves to write, consider teaming up with them (this is not a collaboration, by the way. You are each doing your own separate work). Good writing partners will keep each other motivated and hold each other accountable. Just knowing that you have a reader waiting for your work will help you power through those times when your story is stuck in the mud.

#Stuckbuster

Pro Tips for Writing Partners

- When you choose your writing partner, try to choose someone who not only loves to write as much as you do, but who also won't let you get away with slacking off. Even though they might not show up on your doorstep when you don't turn in your writing, like my writing partner did, you want someone who will at least call you on it.

- You can decide how much writing you can both commit to realistically. It might be a certain number of pages a day or it might be a certain number of words. Don't get too ambitious or you'll risk not being able to keep up. You can decide how many days a week you'll exchange work too. If it's less than seven, I'd suggest naming which days of the week you are going to exchange work. If you're specific it will be easier to keep each other accountable.

- Don't be alarmed if your writing isn't very good, especially at first. In fact, you might find that your writing is . . . um . . . awful. Mine definitely was when we first started exchanging work. Don't be hard on yourself. The point is to be consistent. After you get comfortable with the system, your writing will get better.

- I don't think critiquing each other's work-in-progress is a good idea for writing partners. You are basically exchanging very rough first drafts with each other. Not only is it not super helpful to critique work that is in its early stages, it can also be downright discouraging. The point of having a writing partner is for you to cheer each other on and keep each other writing.

- It might, however, be helpful for you to let each other know which parts of the story you particularly like. You can tell each other which characters you find most intriguing, or which story threads especially interest you.

- If your partner does not give you their writing when they are supposed to, don't let it slide. Give them a little nudge. You want them to do the same for you too. Of course, sometimes life really does get in the way, so be understanding if they have a good excuse.

- Try and help each other to finish the stories. It's a great feeling when you finish a story on your own, but it's even more fun when you have a writing partner who can celebrate with you!

SIXTEEN

#WritingRoutine

I wish I could tell you that the best time to write is from 9 a.m. to 3 p.m. in a south-facing room while wearing a grey hoodie. But I can't. In fact, if someone does tell you stuff like that, don't believe it. There is no magic writing routine. (Although, to be perfectly honest, I'm always rabidly interested in the writing habits of other authors. If they have some cool rituals, I'll always give them a whirl).

The fact is, if you ask twenty successful writers what their workday looks like, you will probably get twenty very different answers. I've known writers who tuck into work at the crack of dawn while propped up on pillows in bed. There are others whose creativity doesn't get revved up until the stars come out. Some writers keep typical nine to five hours in a meticulous office space, while others write whenever, wherever.

What My Writing Day Is Like

After breakfast I head over my computer (unless I'm just starting a book. I write by hand in that case). I have an office in my house but I'll also work on the couch or at the dining room table or in the local café. I'm not fussy.

I open up my story's file and from that point on I use the Bella-style of writing. Bella was my poodle. She was a big scaredy-cat. When faced with a new situation, she'd hide behind me and peer out between my legs. I do the same thing except I use the Internet as the legs. Once my story document is open, I immediately "hide" behind my email. After answering one or two of them, I peek back at my story. Just for a minute or two. Just to reassure myself that it's not as awful as I think it might be. Then I hide again. Maybe this time I'll look at a news story about some guy who found a human finger in his burrito. Then I'll take another peek at my story. I might tap out a sentence or two, in order to test the water, then back to some other bit of distraction. I'll do this for maybe a half hour or so until I feel confident enough to step out behind those legs and get down to work.

Two to three hours of solid writing is a good day for me. I know that doesn't sound like much—lots of other writers clock in far more writing time—but that's usually the most my powers of concentration can withstand. Sometimes, when I'm feeling very sure-footed, I'll go for a longer period of time. When I'm in revision mode, I can work for a whole day, no problem.

I do spend a lot of time thinking about my story, though. I take walks with my dogs and think about what's going to happen next. These thinking-walks are indispensable when I get stuck, too, and I consider them just as important as the actual writing.

*O*bviously, my routine is not going to work for everyone. You might be able to bang out seven- or eight-hours-worth of writing at a time; or perhaps your intense focus enables you to write a decent chunk of work in a single hour. Or maybe you prefer reaching a daily word count. I know one guy who always writes 750 words a day. Why 750? Who knows? But it's his rule and he sticks to it.

#*S*tuckbusters

Writing Habits

- The most important thing is that you commit to some sort of routine. That will help keep you honest. If you don't, it's too easy put off the work when the going gets tough. If you decide that  you work best in the mornings, then commit to that. Set up your "office hours," even if your office is the bathroom. If you decide that your writing hours are 8 a.m. to noon, then plop your butt down somewhere at 8 a.m. and get to work. If you need time to warm up, like I do, build in an extra half hour or so to ease into things.

- Interruptions are a writer's kryptonite. They'll derail you when you are speeding along beautifully, and they'll be an all-too-tempting diversion when you are struggling. You need to take preemptive action against interruptions. If you can, turn off your cell phone. If that's not possible, then only respond to calls and texts that you absolutely have to. Yes, you might irritate a few people who won't understand why you can't spare some time to chat during your writing hours, but they'll just have to get over it. Your writing time is sacred.

- You should also consider interruptions when you decide on a place in which to write. Of course, your own home is the obvious choice. You can use a bedroom or a spare room. Maybe there is an out-of-the-way spot in the house that you could turn into a writing room—like a big closet or an attic. And, hello, the bathroom is one of the best places to write. No one will bother you while you're in there.

- If there are people in your home who just won't respect your privacy, try other writing spots. Libraries are good if you need silence in order to focus. Some people have trouble working when things are too quiet, though. In that case, cafes are great, provided you don't run into anyone you know. Parks can work too. If you travel by train or bus, you can use that as your writing time. I used to have a "floating office": I'd write in the library one day, and the next day a cafe, then the student union at the local university. Speaking of floating offices, I know one author who built herself a raft with a little hut on it. She lets it drift around a cove while she writes—if someone wants to interrupt her, they'll have to do it in their swimsuit.

- If there is a "magic writing routine" it would be this: Wherever you decide to write, and whenever you decide write, just keep showing up. Show up when you are excited about your story and show up when you'd rather step on a pile of Legos in your bare feet than look at the stupid thing again. Show up when you're frustrated or when you're feeling iffy about your skills. Show up when you are horribly, hopelessly stuck. Infinitely more important than *where* you write or *when* you write or how much talent you have is that you just keep writing, no matter what.

SEVENTEEN

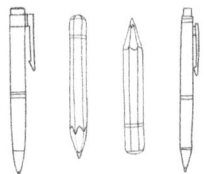

#Collaboration

Bring two writer friends together and sooner or later they will probably consider collaborating on a story. Wouldn't it be much more fun to team up with a pal? It would be half the work and twice the joy, right?

Maybe. A truly great collaboration boils down to finding the right person at the right time. If this sounds like mom's relationship advice, there's a good reason for it. A collaboration is an intense and complicated relationship. A great collaboration can make writing outrageously enjoyable. It can make you a better writer, a better editor, and, yes, even a better person.

However, a bad collaboration can totally blow up in your face. I've heard all sorts of collaboration horror stories. Worst of all, it can cost you a friendship.

Should I Collaborate?

Okay, so let's say you and your friend are considering a collaboration. How do you know if it's a good idea or a terrible one?

The decision to collaborate with someone is as much a gut feeling as anything. I can tell you why Anne Mazer and I collaborated so well together on our book *Spilling Ink, A Young Writer's Handbook*. First of all, we were both very passionate about our project. When Anne suggested writing a handbook for young writers, I felt a little ping in my stomach and couldn't wait to get started! If you and your collaborator are talking a mile-a-minute about the project and practically jumping out of your skin at the thought of writing it, that's a pretty good sign.

Another thing Anne and I had going for us was that we really admired each other's work. That's definitely something to think about before you launch into a collaboration with someone. If you don't like each other's writing now, you are probably not going to like it any better when you work together.

Working Together

While we were collaborating, Anne and I were continuously reading and critiquing each other's pieces. Now this is another place where things could potentially get sticky. Critiquing is always difficult, whether you are giving it or receiving it. Receiving it is probably tougher, so let's start with that.

The first time Anne critiqued one of my sections for *Spilling Ink*, my muscles clenched and I felt my face grow hot. Even before she finished, I wanted to interrupt and defend my work, yet somehow I managed to shut up and listen. When she was done, I thanked her but still felt prickly about it and I was convinced she was wrong. After I calmed down, I read over the changes she had suggested. Very grudgingly, I decided that she was, after all, 100% right. It took several more of these critiques before my muscles unclenched and I began to trust Anne. You may have a similar feeling of resistance, too, when your collaborator critiques you. And hey, the fact is they may be completely wrong about your work. Still, since you've agreed to collaborate with them that probably means you like them and respect their opinion.

If it's so tough to collaborate, you may ask, "Why bother?" Because two people bring double the brain power, double the creativity, and double the obsession to a story. When you get stuck, you have a pal to help unstick you. When you are on your game, your collaborator will encourage you. And on those days when you just don't feel like writing, you push through and do it anyway, because you don't want to disappoint your collaborator. In a nutshell: Great personal chemistry + a shared passion for a story = pure magic. And magic is always worth the bother.

 #*S*tuckbusters

- When you receive a critique, be quiet and listen. Don't rush to defend yourself. Then say "Thank you" because your collaborator has likely spent a lot of time thinking about your work and how to make it better, and that deserves a "Thank you." After that, cool down. Do something else. Clip your toenails, go to the gym, wipe off the gunk between your computer keys. Then go look at your collaborator's comments again. Try them out. If they don't work, fine. If some of the suggestions work and some don't . . . that's also fine. You can make the changes you agree with and explain your reasons for keeping the others as is. And if your collaborator is right on nearly all of the suggestions? Congratulations! You may have just found the person who will help your writing bust loose and soar into the stratosphere.

- When you find yourself in the role of giving a critique, remember how it felt to be on the other side of the equation. How did you respond to your collaborator's critique style? Did you get annoyed when they said, "You should . . ."? Was it easier to hear, "I like what you did, but how about trying . . ."? Be gentle, especially in the beginning when you are both still new to the collaboration. If you start insisting that your way is right, you may make your collaborator give in, but I guarantee that it will annoy them. And guess what? It's your turn to be critiqued next, so look out! They may not be so gentle with you.

- Sometimes, you may launch into a collaboration

that seems great at first; but after a while you begin to question whether it was such a good idea after all. Maybe one collaborator is starting to lose his or her interest in the project. Or your collaborator is getting too bossy. Or you both can't agree on too many issues, or don't find each other's suggestions helpful. There are dozens of reasons why a collaboration that started off well might crumble. Before you throw in the towel, you might try to work things out. Sometimes just bringing the problem out in the open and having an honest chat can help things tremendously. If that doesn't help, though, my feeling is "Friendship over Fiction." Shake hands, hug each other, rub noses, whatever, and tell each other that you gave it your best shot but it just isn't working out. It doesn't mean that you can't try and collaborate again sometime in the future.

STUCK IN THE MIDDLE

EIGHTEEN

#Can'tStopProcrastinating
_____

Writers are total pros when it comes to procrastination. Not only are we trying to do something that is very difficult to do, but we are often doing it on a computer a.k.a. The Procrastination Machine. Come on! That's like someone on a diet working in a donut factory where one of the perks of the job is unlimited donuts.

To make matters even worse, writers are generally very curious people, so they might start wondering what the heck eyebrows are for or what the origin of the word nightmare is (it's from the Old English word "maere" which is a creature that comes into your room at night, holds you down and gives you frightening visions). (I looked that up while procrastinating about writing this section.)

What I'm saying is, don't feel guilty if you're a procrastinator. That's a very common problem for writers. However, just because you shouldn't feel guilty about it, doesn't mean you can't keep procrastination to a minimum. You have stories to tell! No time to waste!

#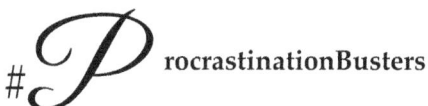rocrastinationBusters

- When I find myself in a procrastination slump, one of my favorite strategies is my Ten-For-Ten Plan. I set a timer and write for ten minutes. When the timer goes off, I stop writing, set the timer for ten minutes again and now I procrastinate. That means I can do anything I like, however bizarre it is. If I feel like watching videos of Bigfoot sightings, that's what I will do. When the timer goes off, I get back to writing again. I'll do this for a solid hour. I find it works amazingly well. Ten minutes is such a short amount of time to write that I almost always feel like I want to go longer. But I can't. When the buzzer goes off I *have* to procrastinate. Forcing yourself to procrastinate takes away some of its glitz and glamour. By the end of the hour, I am usually relieved that I can now just write for longer than ten-minute blocks.

- Get yourself a writing partner. This is such a powerful thing to do, even if you don't have a problem with procrastination (although I know you do!). Guilt is a great motivator, and just knowing that you have a reader anxiously waiting for your work will get you scribbling again.

- Reward yourself. First set a small goal, like finishing a chapter or reaching a word count. Then reward yourself when you attain that goal. The reward could be watching a movie, playing a video game, hanging out with a friend, eating a chocolate bar, posting in social media, or going for a bike ride. That way, you connect something that you are resisting with something you look forward to. After a while, you'll move past the resistance, and the writing will be its own reward.

NINETEEN

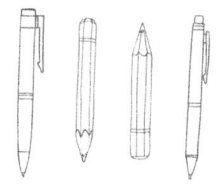

#ImaginationFail
___

I'll bet you were an imagination pro when you were a little kid. Your bicycle was a runaway horse. In the supermarket, you were a CIA operative staking out the shady looking guy in the cereal aisle. Or what about that short, pudgy photographer at Sears? He was actually a gremlin who stole your family when he snapped the family portrait, leaving you with a group of look-alike imposters.

Since you love to write, you probably still have a great imagination. Every so often, though, even writers have an imagination fail. This can happen because you are stressed out or you are trying too hard or because you just haven't written for a while.

When your imagination fails, that movie screen in your mind goes dark. The vivid fictional world you created is now a murky, blobby mess. Your once-alive characters have turned into cardboard cutouts that refuse to do or say anything interesting.

Where did your imagination go?

Realm of Imagination

Recently I was watching a video about fairies for book research (how can you not love a job that requires you to learn about fairies!). When asked why it's always children who claim to see fairies, and hardly ever adults, the "fairy expert" explained that fairies live in a realm between reality and fantasy. Many children, he said, are able to visit that realm easily, but they lose that ability as they get older. Adults can't seem to travel to that realm. Except, he said, for artists, musicians and writers. They still can.

Whether you believe in fairies or not, I do think that the fairy expert was onto something. I think your imagination is not so much a part of your mind, but a place where your mind visits. It's the place where your characters have a pulse and are walking around, full of their own desires and fears and joys. It's the place where your fictional world is buzzing with noise and smells and sensations.

So how can you find your way back to the Realm of Imagination? Well, remember in *Peter Pan* when the children have to cry out, "I do believe in fairies!" in order to keep Tinkerbell from dying? You have to do the same thing. You need to believe it exists.

#Stuckbuster

- I ran a writers' group in my son's school. One day the kids were having trouble focusing so I decided to try something new. I told them to close their eyes. Then I led them through a visualization. I was worried they might be bored, but when it was over they told me that they loved it! Following the visualization, the stories they wrote were unusually vivid. After that, we almost always started our writer's group with a visualization. If I forgot, the kids reminded me.

Below is one of the visualizations I used with my writing group. You or a friend can read it out loud while recording it on some device. Read the script very slowly and in a calm voice. After it's recorded, take your device to a quiet place where no one is likely to bother you. Sit or lie down and make yourself comfortable. Hit play, close your eyes and listen. After it's over, start writing again and see what happens.

ELLEN POTTER

Realm of Imagination Script

Breathe deeply. Slow deep breaths in and out, breathing into your belly. Breath in, breath out.

Breath in, breathe out.

In front of you is a set of stairs. There are ten steps going down. With each step down you are going to feel more and more relaxed. Take the first step. The steps are carpeted and your feet are bare. The carpet feels so soft on your bare feet. You are beginning to relax. Now take the second step down. Feel your arms and legs become loose and relaxed. [Pause.] Take the third step. Breath deeply. [Pause.] Take the fourth step. Your jaw is relaxing and feeling loose. [Pause.] Now walk down to the fifth step. Breath into your belly. [Pause.] Now the sixth step. [Pause.] Now the seventh step. You are feeling very relaxed now. [Pause.] Take the eighth step. [Pause.] Take the ninth step. You are feeling so peaceful. Breathe. [Pause.] Now take the final tenth step. You are totally relaxed.

In front of you is a large golden door. Put your hand on the doorknob. Feel how smooth and cool it is. Open the door and step through it. Look around. Notice everything. Are there trees, or a garden, or is it a city street? What do you hear? What do you smell? Is it warm or cool? Is there a breeze? Is it raining?

In the distance you see movement. Someone or something is approaching. Watch it closely. Is it human? An animal? A mythological creature? As it comes closer, take in all its details. It's standing in front of you now. It hands you something. Look at the object. Turn it over in your hands. Now put it in your pocket. It's yours to keep. Look around one more time. Take three deep breaths. Open your eyes.

When the visualization is over, write a story about the object you put it your pocket and/or the person/creature who gave it to you.

TWENTY

#Perfectionism

A friend of ours came to visit us one summer. Even though he could only stay for a day, we were really excited to see him again. He arrived late in the evening, so we planned on spending the next day doing fun things around town.

In the morning we all had breakfast together, and then our friend said he was going to get himself ready.

We didn't see him again for four hours.

He showered, shaved, exfoliated, tweezed (nose), moisturized, gelled, combed, flossed, clipped (fingers and toes), stretched, and ironed. When he finally emerged he looked great. Like, perfect.

The only problem was, he had spent so much time getting perfect, that he had to head back home just a few hours later.

Why am I telling you this? Because some of you are perfectionists. You know who you are. You get so caught up in primping and buffing and polishing a single chapter or page or even a sentence that you can't move on. You get stuck in an endless loop of reworking the same section over and over. Days, weeks, maybe months go by and your story is just not progressing. Does this sound familiar?

Pobody's Nerfect

Perfectionism is a good news/bad news kind of thing. You already know the bad news—it can paralyze you. It can keep you from ever finishing a single story.

The good news is that there's a time and place for perfectionism. And I should say that by "perfectionism" I mean the desire to make things as perfect as possible, since we all know nothing is perfect.

PERFECTIONISM HAS NO PLACE IN FIRST DRAFTS! ("Ooo, she's using all caps, she must mean it!") I do mean it. First drafts are your baby steps. You wouldn't expect perfection from a baby's first steps, would you? Of course not. First drafts are for you to figure things out, to experiment, to make mistakes. If you could see the first drafts of some of your favorite books, I bet you would be horrified at how awful they are.

Still, once you finish your story and are ready to revise, a healthy dose of perfectionism can be a writer's best friend. Revision is when you want to get all nitpicky. It's when you get to clip and tweeze and buff until you feel your story is gorgeous and ready to face the world.

#*P*erfectionBusters

- Give yourself a limit on how much time you will spend on each chapter (or page or paragraph). Figure out how much time is reasonable. For instance, if I find myself in a rewrite loop on a chapter, I will give myself two more days to work on it. After that, I have to move on to the next chapter no matter what. That might mean there are parts of the chapter that are super rough or not even fully written. I may have to summarize some of it. Too bad. I tell myself I can always go back in and revise.

- Remind yourself that no matter how much you polish up the chapter, you will most likely have to go back in and change things anyway during your revision. I'll say it again—there's no place for perfectionism in first drafts.

- Perfectionism paralyzes creativity. When I find myself obsessing over a section of writing, it feels like a rope is coiling around my imagination, getting tighter and tighter, trapping and restricting it. I can't think creatively. The harder I try to make the section work, the less I'm able to. Once I stop obsessing about the section I'm stuck on and move on to the next section, I feel the rope around my imagination uncoiling. My mind works more fluidly. Ironically, I often figure out how to improve that problematic section once I stop working on it.

- Relax. Do you know what will happen if your

chapter or paragraph or sentence is not perfect? You know what I'm going to say, right? So I'm not even going to say it. I'm going to move on and write the next chapter.

- Okay, I'll say it. *Absolutely nothing.*

TWENTY-ONE

#MyCharactersFeelBlah!

You don't like being pushed around, right? Well neither do your characters. When you force your characters to do things they wouldn't really do, they will cross their arms over their chests, glower at you and refuse to do anything at all. They will make sure you get good and stuck.

Bert The MMA Cage Fighter

For instance, let's say you're writing a story in which Bert, a nerdy teenage hacker, discovers that all his teachers are secretly goblins. And let's say you have mapped out a storyline in which Bert battles with the goblin teachers in the school gym.

You've choreographed the entire fight scene in your outline. Bert does a roundhouse kick to one goblin's ribs, then clobbers another goblin with a badminton racket, lassoes another one with a jump rope, then does a double leg takedown on the last goblin. It's the most exciting scene you've ever outlined!

Except, um . . . Bert is a *nerdy teenage hacker*. How on earth did he suddenly become an MMA cage fighter? If you've taken the time to explore Bert's personality before you started writing (and you really should), you would know that there's no way he would be able to pull off fight moves like that. If you try to force poor Bert to do it, you'll find that your writing will get really awkward and stiff. Bert will become less and less real, until all you'll have left is a stick figure named Bert. Even the most exciting scene will fall flat if your character isn't three dimensional.

So how do you bring your character back to life again?

#Stuckbusters

- Check in with your characters. Even if you've done a lot of work developing them before you started writing the story, it's always a good idea to reconnect with them. If you wrote notes about your characters, go back and look at them. You might have forgotten about some of their qualities. Maybe your character has a phobia of elevators? Or maybe she's proud of her exceptional hand-eye coordination. Reminding yourself of some of your character's quirks, fears, desires, etc., will help you to resuscitate a character who is beginning to fade away or turn two dimensional.

- If you are someone who likes to meticulously map out your story ahead of time, that's fine. Just try not to get too attached to the outline. Sure, you might have made careful plans for your character. You might know ahead of time exactly how they'll act or what they decide to do throughout every step of your story. But stop and consider if those actions and decisions are right for your character. I can hear you saying something like, "But if I change what my character does, the story won't work out the way I want it to." Well, maybe it won't. Maybe it will be even more interesting than what you had planned. Some of my best story lines came from characters behaving in ways that that I hadn't foreseen.

- Remind yourself of your character's deepest desires. One of the most important things you'll do when you are developing a character is to figure out what your character wants. Like *really* wants, more than anything else in the world. That desire, and the fact that you will make it difficult for them to attain it, will drive your story forward. If your character is feeling flat, check in and see if your character's desire is still important in your story. Did your character's desire start out strong, then fizzle? Is there something else that your character wants now? It's okay for your character to change their desires (that happens to all of us sometimes), as long as you can keep the new desire front and center in the story.

- Write a journal entry in your character's voice. You can write their observations about other characters, their feelings about events that occur in the story, or simply let them ramble on and see where their thoughts go. I often do this when I feel like I'm losing my grasp on a character. It always helps me to slip inside their mind and hear their voice—and I'm sometimes shocked at what I find out about them.

TWENTY-TWO

#InternetDistraction!
_____

My poodle Bella had some peeing issues. She would find the right spot, squat down . . . but wait! What's coming down the street? Another dog? *Boom*! She forgot all about peeing. After the dog passed by, she found another spot that seemed pee-worthy, squatted . . . but wait! Is that a Cheetos bag blowing across the grass? And once again, she forgot all about peeing. If there were enough distractions, she could have twenty false starts before she actually did her business.

Was she a scatterbrain nut job? Yes she was. But let's be honest, how many of you have started working on your story only to get distracted by an email alert? And then you start writing again, only to realize you need to Google "Birthday Cake-flavored Oreo cookies vs. Brownie Batter Oreos." Fast forward to an hour later, and you've forgotten to go back to writing your story altogether. At least Bella eventually remembered to pee.

#Writers911

Annoying Friend at the Movies

Look, I love the Internet. But I hate the Internet too. It can sidetrack writers like nothing else. For one thing, it makes procrastination all too easy. When you're feeling the discomfort of being stuck in your story, you can pick up your phone and check out your friend's new Jordans instead. It's just so tempting! I get that.

Still, a big part of writing is feeling that squirmy, uncomfortable sensation you experience when you don't know what happens next in your story, or when your plot is spinning out of control. The discomfort is there for a reason: it's urging you to find a solution. If you keep numbing it with Google searches or social media, you'll never get unstuck.

Here's another reason that too much Internet stinks for writers—it just won't shut up! Writers create new worlds, and in order to do that we need *this* world to leave us alone for a while. Imagine watching a movie in a theater with a friend, and that friend keeps whispering comments in your ear. Can you concentrate on the movie? Well, maybe between comments. But you definitely can't lose yourself in the movie in the same way you can when no one is talking to you. All those pinging phones and ringing apps and beeping computers are like that annoying friend. Good luck creating worlds with all that racket!

Me Eat Brains

I know it's hard to resist peeking at those alerts. After all, they might mean that something exciting is happening. The next time you're writing and you hear a little *pa-ping!* or a *chirp!*, here's what you need to say to yourself: "There is no alert that is as amazing as the feeling I'm going to get when I finish writing this story." That is the truth. Sure, you might get a quick rush of *whoa!* when the kid you like from algebra class "follows" you on social media. Yes, you might get a laugh at seeing the selfie of your friend with a pig snout. That's reacting to things. Nothing feels as great as creating something. NOTHING. It changes you forever.

Want to know the scariest thing about the Internet? It might be changing our brains in a way that is especially bad for writers. Yes, there has been research done on this (you can Google it, but wait until you get to the end of this section). The frenzied movements from one subject to another may limit your ability to focus and think deeply. I've found if I am very active on the Internet, especially if I'm messing around rather than using it for serious information gathering, my creativity tanks. I can't think deeply. The words—and the worlds—don't form easily. Writers thrive on slow, deep thought. If we're not careful, too much Internet can chew up and swallow the deep-thinking portions of our brains. The zombie apocalypse is no joke, folks.

#Stuckbusters

- Go old school. Use a pen and

paper to write your story. If you
are an office supply geek like me,
you might get inspired by
purchasing a really great
notebook and a pen that writes
like liquid silk (yeah, I said it.
Liquid silk.) This will help keep
you away from the Internet, and, as an added
bonus, writing by hand may boost your creativity.

- Instead of Googling things for research as you're writing (which may lead to falling down those rabbit-hole distractions), jot down all the little things you'll need to research and then Google them later. You can insert a question mark beside the places in your story that need some Internet help, or highlight it, or use your own special code. This way you can do all your research at once without interrupting your focus during writing time.

- Chunk it up. If going without Internet for a long period of time makes you jittery, give yourself time limits. You can set a timer for a half hour, then turn off your Internet access (and remember to shut off that phone too—no cheating) and try writing without it for a half hour. Then give yourself a half hour online, then again, a half hour off to write. I notice when I do that, I gradually lose interest in finding out which movie star is getting a divorce and become more interested in my own story.

- If you don't trust your self-control, there are apps to keep you honest and internet free for a set period of time.

- If you have a writing partner, you can make an accountability pact with each other where you promise to only spend a certain amount of time on the Internet.

- Okay, now you can Google "What the Internet does to your brain."

TWENTY-THREE

#StuckAgain!What'sWrongWithMe?

There is nothing wrong with you! Writing is hard. Sure, there are times when the words pour out of you; but there are also times—many times—when they trickle out in spits and spurts like a garden hose with a kink in it. That's when many writers start questioning themselves. They might wonder if they have what it takes to be a writer; if they are smart enough or creative enough. "If I had real talent," they might think, "I'd be breezing through this story. I'd never get this frustrated or feel this lost."

The Writer Store

When it all shakes out, raw talent isn't as important as you might think. I've known some very gifted writers who were unable to finish a single story. If there were a "Writer's Store" where you could purchase any trait you wanted, I'd buy "Persistence" over "Natural Talent" each and every time.

A persistent writer finishes the story they start, and then has the bulldoggedness to go back and revise it a dozen times or more.

A persistent writer struggles through the rough patches, even when they feel like feeding the whole story to a shredder, then torching the scraps for good measure. And, slowly but surely, a persistent writer can become a talented writer. If you put in the hours, the passion, and the focus, chances are you will evolve into a writer with some real skills.

The Big, Scary Adventure

And now for the bad news (don't worry, it's good news too): It doesn't get any easier. Ever. Seriously.

Each story you write is going to give you a major headache at some point. Even now, after having written twenty books, I am still shocked that this whole writing gig is not getting easier. In fact, when I recently complained to a friend that the book I was currently working on was the hardest book I'd ever written, my friend snorted and said, "You say that about all your books!"

Yikes! She was right.

It makes sense though. With each new story, you are freshly conjuring worlds out of thin air. You are populating those worlds with people who don't exist, and breathing life into storylines that need to enthrall your readers, page after page. That's some big, scary stuff. But it's also part of the adventure of writing.

Every time you sit down to write a new story, go in expecting trouble. But also go in knowing that the synapses in your brain are going to be lighting up like fireworks, and that you will be absorbed into a fantastic world that you have imagined into existence. What a feat! What a thrill!

And yes, on occasion, what torture!

But that's okay. It's all part of the adventure.

#Stuckbuster

Well, this isn't so much a Stuckbuster as a story I wanted to tell you. It's a true story about a seal. Stick with me, this *is* going somewhere . . .

A few years ago, I lived in a tiny village on the coast of Maine. One summer I started to notice some posts on my Facebook page from Eve, a woman who worked in our local convenience store. Eve was posting photos of a seal she called Sammy. She said that Sammy lived in the harbor, by the village dock, and whenever Eve called his name, he popped his head up out of the water, swam right up to her, and let her pet him.

Wow! I thought. That's amazing!

I also didn't really believe it. So the next time I was in the convenience store, I asked Eve about it. This is what she told me:

"Five years ago, I was walking by the town dock one evening and I saw this young seal playing in the water. I named him Sammy. I don't know why. He just looked like a Sammy. After that, I would go to the dock every evening to see if Sammy was there. I'd call out his name and sometimes he would pop his head out of the water, but plenty of times he wouldn't. I just kept going there every single night and calling his name. There were times when I wouldn't see him for weeks and I would worry that something bad had happened to him. But then he'd just show up one day out of the blue. After a while he began to show up more and more until finally I could go out to the dock every evening, call out "Sammy!" and he'd be there, like he was expecting me. If the tide is high, I can sit on the dock with my legs in the water, and when I call him, he swims over and nuzzles my legs and lets me pet him. Other people have tried to call him, but he only comes to my voice."

Holy Andre the Seal! I love that story! For one thing, it's just downright awesome to be friends with a wild seal. But I also love this story because it contains great advice for writers (see, I told you to stick with me). Just like Eve, writers have to keep showing up. Every day you have to sit down with your computer or a notebook and spend time with your story. Yes, sometimes nothing happens. You can't think of a single thing to write. Inspiration is somewhere far out at sea and no matter how much you may want it to come to you, it refuses to surface. But you have to keep showing up anyway, day after day. If possible, try to show up at the same time of day and the same place, just like Eve did, so that Inspiration knows when and where to find you. Eventually, it will return to you. Inspiration loves persistence.

Apparently, so do seals.

TWENTY-FOUR

#Copycat

We're all natural-born imitators. When we were toddlers we learned to walk and talk and spoon up mushy peas by imitating people who were better at it than we were. The same goes for writing. We learn how to write by noticing how other people do it. In fact, no books or stories are totally original. They have all, to some extent, been influenced by books that have come before them.

Valerie's Ducks

There is a big difference, though, between being influenced by a book and copying from it. You know the difference. You do. You learned all about it when you were seven or eight. Remember sitting next to that kid—let's call her Valerie—who could draw a really great duck swimming in a pond. You thought it was so cool that you started drawing a duck swimming in a pond, too, until Valerie accused you of being a copycat. She was right. But having learned how to draw a duck in a pond you then started to experiment. Your pond expanded into an ocean and the duck morphed into a gull, then a sailboat, and then a pirate ship. Before long you could sit next to Valerie, draw your pirate ship on the ocean, and she would look over at it and say, "Hey, nice drawing." You had moved from imitation to inspiration.

Imitation vs. Inspiration

How do you know if you are inspired by something or are simply being a copycat?

You'll probably be able to feel it. If, for instance, you don't feel confident in your own work unless you keep referring to someone else's as you are writing, whether it's by flipping through the book or mentally referring to it, you are probably being a copycat.

On the other hand, when you're influenced by another writer, you may use some of their techniques or themes— maybe you love the dry humor of a particular author's dialogue or the way a certain book can make your skin crawl with scenes of horror—but you are first and foremost immersed in your *own* story. It's your own voice, not someone else's, that shines through your writing.

Imitating can be a tempting habit, whether it's because the book you are imitating is a mega-best-seller ("If I just imitate this book, a publisher will snap up my manuscript and I'll be a billionaire in no time") or simply because you admire an author. Ultimately, though it's a bad idea. For one thing, your imitation won't be as good as the original; and for another, it will cause you to lose faith in yourself as a writer. Writing fiction is all about weaving your own unique experiences and visions into something fresh for your readers. To fake it is to miss out on the adventure of exploring your own imagination.

The Evil Book Worm

Is there a book you love so much that you've read it seven times? Can you quote passages from it, and in fact do so pretty often, much to the annoyance of your friends? Every time you sit down to write, do parts of that book seem to seep into your characters, your dialogue, your storyline? Congratulations, my friend, you have yourself a "book worm," which is the writing equivalent of an "ear worm" (that song that gets stuck in your head). So what do you do if you have a book worm? Read on . . .

\#Stuckbusters

- Let's say the book worm is a certain dystopian novel. The first thing you have to do is to stop reading it. I mean it. Hide it

behind your other books on the bookshelf, take it off your Kindle, whatever. Now go to the library and check out a bunch of other dystopian novels that look interesting. The idea is to dilute the intensity of your beloved book. Reading other books in the genre can help shake loose your own imagination from the grip of the book worm. You might find that there are other writers you admire. Their work might spark new story ideas or qualities in your characters. If you read widely you are less likely to become fixated on a single book, and less likely to become a copycat.

- One of the best ways to avoid being a copycat is to try to figure out what it is that you love about an author's style or a particular storyline. Pick it apart and analyze it. Do you love an author's main character? Ask yourself which of the character's qualities fascinate you. Break them down into bite-sized pieces: His adorable near-sightedness; the way he gave his coat to his little sister; his inability to talk to the checkout girl at Wal-Mart. Then see if you can transfer those qualities to one of your own characters. For example, kindness to a younger sister can be translated into a moment of tenderness for a vulnerable friend. That near-sightedness can become a food allergy. As you begin to veer off from the piece that you are imitating, you will find that your work will start to breathe on its own.

- When you imitate someone else, you are essentially saying, "I can't do this on my own." But you can. In fact, you probably already have. Gather up a few of your own stories, sit back, and read them as though they aren't yours. What do you like most about them? Do you have clean, spare descriptions? A great grasp of realistic dialogue? Are you especially inventive? Try to see the things that make your writing unique. If it's too hard for you to be objective, give the stories to a trusted friend and ask them what they like best. Once you've identified your strengths, use them! Delight your readers with those impressive descriptive skills. Apply your gift for dialogue to develop your characters more deeply. Take your natural skillset and see if you can improve it. Paying attention to the things you do well will help keep your focus where it should be—on your own work rather than on someone else's.

TWENTY-FIVE

#BoredOfMyStory

Sometimes when you've worked out your whole story ahead of time—all the plot twists all the drama—you might feel too bored or uninspired to write it.

First of all, don't be so sure that you do know the whole story. When you wake up in the morning, you often "know" what you'll be doing that day, right? Yet there are always surprises that pop up—you might run out of shampoo and while you're in the drug store buying a bottle, you bump into your archenemy from first grade. Or you find a twenty-dollar bill poking out of a snow bank. Or maybe you witness a car accident downtown. Unexpected things happen in real life. They can happen in your story too.

Ramon And The Necromancer

Let's say that you have carefully plotted out the chapter in which Ramon is on his way to a necromancer who will raise the spirit of his dead sister. Pretty exciting stuff. Yet if you, the writer, already know that Ramon's sister is not really dead but is being held prisoner by the necromancer, writing this cool storyline may feel very blah. But something unexpected can always happen. Maybe on his way to the necromancer, Ramon sees a young woman about to leap to her death into the icy bay. He stops and persuades her not to, and in the process finds that she has a shadowy connection with the necromancer. Okay, now things are getting a little more interesting for you.

Don't be afraid to veer off a little from your outline. Maybe you'll want to make a total detour. Remember, *your plot outline is not the boss of you*. It can help you gain a footing in your story when you first start to write it, but you may have to hike through several chapters before you get a solid feel for your fictional world. That's when you can loosen your death grip on the plot outline. Let unplanned events slip into your story. Let your characters make decisions you hadn't predicted, and follow the consequences of those decisions to see where they take you.

The Piranha Infested Lagoon

If you want, you can take this a step farther by not plotting out your story at all. Or you could do just a smidgen of plotting, which is how I like to write.

When I begin a story, my focus is squarely on the characters. I often have a general idea of their situation and/or dilemma, but not much more than that. I like to give the story space to tell itself and to let my characters make impromptu decisions as events unfold.

Now, I'm not going to lie—writing without meticulously outlining the plot ahead of time can be nerve-wracking. It will sometimes feel like you are pawing around in the dark on the extra-slippery banks of a piranha-infested lagoon. You will follow some storylines that will lead you nowhere and you'll inevitably have to scrap a chapter . . . or two or three or four. But the payoff can be tremendous. You are giving your story permission to be spontaneous, to behave like "real life," in all its glorious unpredictability. When you write this way, as scary as it is, you will surprise and delight yourself with unexpected twists and turns in the plot. And if you're surprised and delighted, just imagine how your readers will feel.

#Writers911

lotbusters

- **The Old Switcheroo**

When you feel too locked into your plot and want to shake things up, try switching your story's point-of-view. A different POV will give you a fresh perspective on a scene or a character. You may also stumble upon a new plot thread that fascinates you and brings back that feeling of excitement you initially had for your story. Try it. After doing this exercise, you may decide to change the perspective in the story, or to have more than one person narrate the story. Even if you decide to keep things as they are, you will have seen your story through new eyes and that might be enough to banish the boredom.

- **The Unexpected Road**

When I lived in upstate New York there was a road that my son and I used to love to drive down. We called it The Unexpected Road because we always encountered the most unusual things when we travelled on it—a little Amish boy walking a giant horse like it was a dog, a hawk flying overhead with a rabbit in its talons, a snowman with a bra on it. When you are getting bored with your story, take a detour down the Unexpected Road. Lose the outline and follow the storyline that makes your blood run a little faster. Start thinking "What if . . .?" What if the snowboarding girlfriend who dies in an avalanche actually survives? What if your character doesn't get that cushy summer internship and instead has to wait tables at the local diner? Try it out. See if something remarkable happens. If you hate it, well, that's what the Delete key is for. Or even better, save the draft in case you change your mind later.

- **Character Study**

Reconnect with your characters. If you interviewed your characters (see #CreatingGreatCharacters) take a look at the what your characters "said." You may have forgotten some of their key qualities that will change the direction of the story. If, for instance, your main character said they were afraid of drowning, then their decision to walk across a frozen lake to escape from a kidnapper will take on an extra layer of suspense. The character may have to wrestle with their inner demons before they make the decision to escape. Or they may choose not to escape if their fear of drowning is too great. Or perhaps the kidnapper knows about this fear, which is why he chose to keep her on an island. Reconnecting with your characters will help you to see if you've forgotten something crucial about their personality or history that might add a whole new dimension to your plot and make you fall in love with your story all over again.

TWENTY-SIX

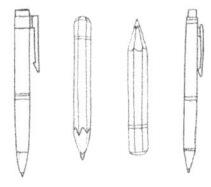

#Secrets&Lies
_____

"I know a secret."

Four little words. That's all it takes to make people stop whatever it is they're doing and pay attention. That's some powerful stuff and writers know it. Nothing can sweep a reader into a story and keep them reading until the wee hours of the morning like a really juicy secret.

Of course, interesting stories begin with interesting characters. Even the juiciest secret will lose its juice without great characters to keep it or wonder about it or unearth it. But if you have created characters that feel alive and dynamic, and you are looking for another way to deepen the interest in your storyline, you might consider weaving a secret into your main plot or a subplot. Maybe your main character's brother murdered someone. Or your character talks to ghosts. Or your character is actually not human.

Secretbusters

- Let it subtly slip that your character has a secret.

- Now that you've let it slip, your job is to keep the secret. I know that seems obvious, but it's actually harder than you might think, and here's why: As the story progresses, the secret needs to be unearthed a bit. Your readers are excavating as they are reading, and you'll want them to find a fragment or two of something promising in order to encourage them to keep digging. It might be a physical object. It might be something that a character says. It might be a simple gut feeling that your character has. Whatever it is, it must be enticing yet still maddeningly puzzling.

- Make sure that the pursuit of the secret is at least as interesting as the secret itself. Now this is crucial because, unlike real life, your readers can simply flip to the end of the book to find out what the secret is. So how do you help your readers sustain that breathless "Leave me alone, can't you see I'm reading!" interest in the pursuit? Well, a big part of it is making sure that you, the writer, are just as interested in the pursuit as the reader. This isn't easy, since you already know the secret, right? That's when you have to take the Lawn Mower Dude approach. What's that? Read on . . .

Lawn Mower Dude

A friend of mine drove across the country with just maps. She refused to use GPS. Whenever she got lost, she stopped a dude who was mowing his lawn (in every town across the nation, there is always a dude mowing his lawn) and asked for directions. Sometimes Lawn Mower Dude gave her good directions; and sometimes she wound up at an alpaca farm or a gum ball factory. That suited her just fine. Yes, she wanted to reach her destination; but she also wanted to see some interesting stuff along the way. When writing about a secret, leave the GPS at home and keep an open mind. While it's good to know where you're going, be willing to take some back roads. Let yourself be surprised by odd twists and turns in the storyline that you haven't mapped out ahead of time.

While I was writing *The Humming Room*, a contemporary retelling of the classic book *The Secret Garden*, I knew that there had to be a hidden garden in my novel. How on earth was I supposed to captivate my readers, and myself, with a secret that most of us already knew?

Oh yeah. Lawn Mower Dude.

The "back road" I followed was the main character, Roo. A half-wild girl from a violent home, she has a talent for hiding *Bam!* There was my interesting detour: This girl can find secret places. Not only does she find the garden, but she finds other things as well . . . a mysterious boy who may or may not be human; a box of treasures hidden by a dying girl; the source of the eerie humming in the house. Yes, she finds the secret garden too, but in the process she has so many other adventures that (I hope) readers forget that they already know the secret.

TWENTY-SEVEN

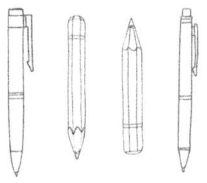

#FreakyFactor

The more you write, the more you may notice weird things happening. No, it's not your imagination. Writing can be spooky. For instance, you'll be writing about a power outage in your character's house, and suddenly the lights in your own house will flicker. Or you just wrote a scene in which a guy takes someone hostage at the grocery store and that night you read a news story about a guy who takes a hostage at a grocery store. No kidding, this kind of thing tends to happen to writers. Why? Honestly, I'm not sure.

I have noticed that weird coincidences happen when I'm fiercely focused on my work. Maybe the deep concentration allows you to see the invisible threads that connect the Fictional World with the Everyday World. Or maybe it brings on episodes of clairvoyance. But don't quote me on that. All I know is that many of my writer friends have experienced this type of synchronicity, too, which makes me think there really is something to it.

The Spooky Stuff

When I first started experiencing the spooky stuff, they were simply fun stories to tell at parties: "The strangest thing just happened to me. The week after I finished writing a story about a girl who takes her depressed mathematician brother on a road trip to Niagara Falls, I met a girl who had just come back from Niagara Falls with her brother. Oh and by the way, he was a math major who was battling depression." (True story!)

After a while, though, I began to wonder if these fluky events could be something that I could tap into deliberately. So I began to experiment. When I found myself impossibly stuck on a scene, I would stop writing and go about my day, all the while keeping an eye out for helpful "coincidences." It was like being on a paranormal scavenger hunt. Lo and behold, I'd overhear a conversation that seemed tailor-made for my story. Or I'd spot an object—once it was a picture of a gondola, another time a miniature house carved out of wood—that gave me a powerful blast of inspiration. They're like little gifts dropped from the sky. Personally, I like to think that there is a Heavenly Council of Dead Writers who take pity on us struggling living writers and toss a few clues our way.

Heavenly Council of Dead Writers

The best thing is, you don't even need to be awake to tap into the spooky stuff. When something in my story is driving me nuts, I take the problem to bed with me. I close my eyes and think about the aggravating character or not-quite-right storyline. Sometimes I wake up in the morning and I'm still aggravated. Then I have to try again. Many times, though, I wake up and . . . *blammo!* I have a brilliant insight or I remember a dream that hands me the answer to my problem.

For instance, when I was writing my middle-grade novel *SLOB,* I couldn't figure out which character was stealing from my narrator and making his life a nightmare. I had a cast full of suspects, but no idea "who done it." So I went to bed with the question of the mystery thief firmly lodged in my brain. That night I dreamt that my brother was furious at me for something. I woke up frazzled and upset, even though I knew that my brother wasn't really mad at me; I had just spoken to him on the phone a few days before. In a flash, I realized that the dream was an answer to my question. My narrator had a sister. She hadn't been on my list of suspects, but she had the motive and the means. She made perfect sense. The thief was the narrator's sister! Thank you, Heavenly Council of Dead Writers! May the coffee always be hot and strong in that Starbucks in the sky!

#Stuckbusters

- If you have already noticed the spooky stuff, congratulations! Now you can start experimenting with it. Ask it for help when you are stuck, then keep your eyes and ears on high alert. Don't dismiss things that seem to flag you. Let your mind play with them. See if they can shed some light on your story or send your brain in a new direction. These little gifts can appear in the form of a conversation overheard in McDonald's, an image on a coffee mug, the smell of sunscreen, the face of a bus driver, signs on a building, text messages. You get the idea. Anything.

- Another approach is to think about your writing problems before you go to sleep. No stress; keep it casual. Tell yourself you'll wake up with an answer. Then let Jane Austen and William Shakespeare do some brainstorming on your behalf (or feel free to take full credit for your brilliant unconscious mind).

- A word of warning: You can't always count on the spooky stuff to come through for you. I've noticed that it favors the obsessed. When I'm just noodling around, it's nowhere in sight. But once I plunge into a story with gusto, the spooky stuff steps up and starts doing its thing.

- Now if you have never experienced anything spooky, it could be that you just haven't noticed it. Or maybe it hasn't happened to you yet. Maybe it never will. It doesn't mean that you are doing anything wrong as a writer. Some writers experience this and some don't. Still, now that you know that it *could* happen, you won't think you're going bonkers if it does.

TWENTY-EIGHT

#MessyPlot

I've observed that there are two different types of people in this world: those who don't mind untangling impossibly knotted shoelaces and those who prefer to snip off the laces, toss them in the trash, and start with a fresh pair.

I'm a snipper. Untangling things gives me a low-grade fever. That's why I've had to think a lot about how to untangle knotty stories, because, frankly, if I tossed out my stories whenever they got snarled up, I'd never have finished a single one.

Getting Into The Mess

A tangle isn't necessarily a bad thing. In fact, it's often a sign that you've been hard at work. Tangles usually—but not always—happen when you have been working on a story over a long period of time. You may have woven in so many subplots that you've lost track of them; or perhaps your characters made some choices along the way that have twisted your storyline into a pretzel; or maybe you've veered off so dramatically from your original idea that the story no longer makes sense.

When you find yourself in a muddle like this, the temptation is to just toss the manuscript out and start all over again.

Snip, snip.

Before you do that, though, it's worth your while to try to figure out why things got all twisted up in the first place. Because, as my mother used to say, "If you were able to get into this mess, you're able to get out of it too."

Getting Out Of The Mess

If you watch those people who are good at unknotting shoelaces, you may notice that before they even tug on a single lace, they examine the snarl. They try to see where things went wrong. It's wise to take that approach with your writing as well. The first thing you need to do is . . . nothing. If you impatiently start ripping apart your story in order to fix it, you'll probably wind up with a nastier tangle. Instead, take a breath. Don't panic. Go back and read the story from the beginning. Try to enjoy what you've written—there's bound to be lots of good stuff in there. Appreciating the parts that are working will help you to spot the parts that aren't.

Personally, when I hit the sections in my story that aren't

quite right, I feel squirmy and anxious. You may have a different method of knowing. Pay attention to your gut reactions. They'll give you information on when your story has gone wrong.

Here are some ideas to help you untangle those knots.

#Stuckbusters

- Print out your story then cut it up. Snip out the separate story lines so you can see exactly what you've written. This will give you clear visual clues as to what your story is made of. Once  you've sorted that out, you can decide to rearrange or discard sections. You might even find that you have two—or more—separate stories in one.

- Ask yourself: Why did I want to write this story in the first place? What was it about the story that excited me the most? Was it a situation? A character? A theme I wanted to explore? Reread your story from the beginning and see if it's veered off from your original motivation. If it has, take note of the parts of the story that stayed the course; they might be the keepers while the other bits are the ones to file away for another story.

- No doubt about it, subplots help keep things interesting. They add layers, complications and resonance to your main plot. Still, too many subplots can smother the core story, so check if your subplots are adding anything to the main story. If they aren't, you should probably cut them.

- If a particular subplot seems to be dominating the main plot, maybe that subplot is actually more interesting to you than the core story. That's totally fine. In fact, it happens quite often. If that's the case, consider rerouting your story so that the subplot is the main storyline. The fact is, if you're losing interest in the original storyline, your readers will too. True, rerouting the story will mean more work for you, but—look out, I'm going to quote my mother again—"If it's worth doing, it's worth doing well."

- If you're writing a very complicated storyline, check out fiction writing software. I resisted using these tools for many years, but now I find them to be pretty helpful. Some of the better fiction writing software can help you tease out your different story threads and keep them organized. I use Scrivener but there are many other good ones.

- Juggling a lot of characters in your book can cause a nice little snarl. Characters have a way of accumulating, particularly when you have been working on a story for a long time. Make sure that all your characters are well defined. Check that each character's description, the choices that they make, and their dialogue make them pop as a unique individual. Also check to see that all your characters are necessary for the story to move forward. If you did away with Uncle Frank, would the plot suffer? If not, well, you know what to do with him.

STUCK AT THE END

TWENTY-NINE

#UnfinishedStories
___

Why is it so hard to finish a story?
I have a theory.
But before I tell you what it is, think about how you feel when you have a crush on someone. You get dizzy with excitement. You think about the person every minute of the day. You imagine a gorgeous, shimmering, arm-in-arm future with your crush.

Then you start dating that person, and . . . *hmm*. You begin to discover some less-than-shimmering qualities in your crush. Maybe the person is a die-hard collector of Pokémon cards. Or maybe their personal hygiene leaves something to be desired. Before long, the relationship shrivels up and dies.

The Break-Up

When you first start writing a story, you are essentially in the wild throes of a crush. You are consumed with your fictional world and the characters that live there. The first pages always seem to flow out effortlessly. The writing feels charmed. But the more you write, the more you deepen your relationship with your story. That's when you start to notice that things aren't as perfect as you first thought. That's when many people stop writing. That's when they "break up" with their story.

"I think we should stop seeing each other for a little while," you tell your crush/story-in-progress. "Maybe just for a week or so."

Fast-forward to a year and that story-in-progress is still untouched.

Now just as not all crushes are good relationship material, not all stories or novels should be finished. But they should at least be given a fighting chance.

Here are some things you can do to rekindle your relationship with the unfinished story . . .

#Stuckbusters

- Make a date with your story. Take it out of the closet or wherever it is hidden. Read it. And that's all. Sounds simple, I know, but it actually takes some guts to do this.

- Allow yourself to (possibly) fall in love again. Sometimes just the act of rereading a story can help you to remember all the things you loved about it in the first place. Yes, you'll also probably see the parts that make you squirm. But maybe, just maybe, you'll find that the good parts outweigh the bad.

- Remember, nobody's perfect. This goes double for works of fiction. Stories and novels are nearly always troublesome things. They hardly ever do what you want them to do (at least not for very long). The good news is that when you haven't looked at a story for a while, solutions to the problem areas may jump right out at you. It may be as simple as deleting a scene or changing its outcome.

- Make a fresh start. Take your story to a romantic place it's never been before. You could write in a tree house, in a museum, by the light of a campfire, or even in a closet. Shake things up and see what happens.

- Flirt with your story. Be playful. Skip over the boring parts and go straight for the juicy bits. Move scenes around, add a sizzling new character, or try writing from a different point of view. Just mess around and have fun.

- Fight for it. Let's say you have reconnected with your old story. And you've fallen in love again. And all those things that were giving you problems before have now been sorted out. Fantastic! I

#Writers911

couldn't be happier for you. Still—and I hate to be a joy-buster here—you are probably going to run into trouble with your story again before long. It's just the way things go in this writing business. If it were easy, there wouldn't be billions of unfinished stories out there, right?

- When you come to those problem spots, it might be tempting to break up with your story again, especially since there's always a new, hotter-looking story idea beckoning to you from across the street. But you know what? You're going to have relationship issues with that hot new story too. The fact is that nearly every novel I have ever written has made me want to tear my hair out at some point. When you come up against those disturbing moments—like discovering that your crush has a stash of Pokémon cards in acid-free albums—try and stick with it. See if you can work things out. You might just have a brilliant novel on your hands. And you also might discover that you are weirdly fond of Pikachu.

- If, after all your best efforts, the story is still going nowhere, it may be time to call it quits. It's possible that you and your story are just not meant to be. No hard feelings. You can toss or delete your story, or tuck it back in your closet (after all, there could still be a few gorgeous sentences in it that you might want to use later). And uh oh . . . don't look now, but I think there's a smoking-hot story idea checking you out.

THIRTY

#WhatWillPeopleThink?!
___

Whenever you put your words out into the world, you are bound to make a few people angry, or become the target of a sneer or two.

I'm tempted to tell you, "Don't waste a second of your time worrying about that nonsense." And while that is the truth, I also know it's not quite so easy. When people don't approve of or make fun of your work, it can feel like an attack on your very soul.

Don't Fear The Sneer

Now to be clear, we're not talking about someone who just doesn't like your work. You may not be happy that they didn't like it, but I'm sure you've read books or stories that just didn't do it for you either. There's criticism meant to make your story better; and then there's criticism meant to make you feel bad for having written the story in the first place.

Maybe someone doesn't approve of the fact that one of your characters behaves immorally. Or maybe someone makes fun of an especially sentimental moment. Shaming criticism is designed to pressure you into changing what you write, how you think, or even into not writing at all. If you worry about how your story will affect certain people (assuming, of course, that you are not writing directly about them without disguising their identity) that will paralyze you on the spot. It's your job as a writer to let your story go to all those places it needs to go, even if it might be uncomfortable for some of your readers. When you change your voice in order to please other people, the only thing you will succeed in doing is to suck all the joy out of writing, and we can't have that.

#Stuckbusters

- Remember this: Almost all the world's finest writers were ridiculed for their work at one time or another. Mark Twain once said this about Jane Austen: "Every time I read *Pride and Prejudice*, I want to dig her up and hit her over the skull with her own shin-bone." Which is sort of funny, but mean nonetheless.

- Believe this: When you write with honesty and bravery, you will win more hearts than you will lose.

- When you are finished with your story, be choosy about who gets to read it. If you suspect that a certain person will disapprove or make fun of it, don't let them read it unless they absolutely need to. You should definitely refrain from letting those people read it before it's done. A negative reaction to a work-in-progress can crush your confidence and stop your momentum.

- If you feel you have to show your work to a potentially disapproving person, help them to frame their response to it. For instance, you could say, "Heads up, there's a scene on page five that you might not approve of, but I'd love to hear what you think of the story as a whole." That might help to defuse their reaction, and who knows . . . they may think the story is pitch-perfect just as it is.

- If a certain person's disapproving face keeps looming up menacingly as you are trying to write, thank them. You know why? Because they are teaching you how to be brave, and let me tell you, writing is not for the spineless.

THIRTY-ONE

#TheEnd?

You are nearly done with your story! Can you believe it?! You've wrestled with those rough patches, gotten stuck and unstuck a dozen times or more. Though you were tempted to trash your story a few times, you wisely decided to power through instead.

By now, your brain is probably more deep-fried than a corndog. You might be tempted to scribble the first ending that comes into your head just so you can wrap things up.

Don't.

Endings can make or break your story. They can be the difference between a story with the staying power of a soap bubble and one that readers just can't stop thinking about. Hey, you've already made it this far, so don't poop out in the final lap. Take a deep breath. Good. Now let's dig in and find the perfect ending.

First check whether you have already ended the book without realizing it. Weird as that sounds, it does happen quite often. You were so busy worrying about how to end the story that you didn't even notice you wrote the perfect ending three chapters back. Boy, I love when that happens! Look for that easy fix before you do anything else.

If you haven't already ended the story, the best thing you can do is to read the whole manuscript from the beginning. You want the story to be fresh in your mind before you work out the ending. Once you've reread your story, try these . . .

#Stuckbusters

- Sometimes you can find your ending by looking at your beginning. Endings that echo something at the beginning can be very satisfying. Maybe your character does the same thing at the end that she did in the beginning, only now, having been changed by events in the story, her action or reaction is different. For instance, you may have started your story like this:

At the age of eighteen, the riskiest thing Brenda McCoy had ever done was to take an aspirin without water.

But as the story goes on, Brenda might be faced with some dangerous situations. Her experiences change her. An ending that underscores this change, and echoes the beginning, might be perfect . . .

Bruised from her fight and badly scraped by the tumble off the roof, Brenda collapsed onto her girlfriend's couch and groaned in pain.
   'I have some aspirin,' her girlfriend offered.
   'Fine,' Brenda murmured. 'I'll take two. No water.'

- Consider the tone of your ending. It will provide your story with an echo that will reverberate in your reader's head after they've finished. Are you shooting for a happy, "everything-turned-out-perfectly" sort of ending? Or perhaps the fairy tale ending isn't right for your story. An ending in which you show how your character has changed because of events in the story can feel more layered. Endings that are surprising are another option, but you have to make sure that you don't sacrifice logic for shock value. If your honest, sweet-natured barista turns out to be a crooked CIA agent, there had better be some evidence in the book that makes this believable or your readers will be very annoyed with you.

- Ask yourself if the ending makes sense. Be honest. If you were impatient to end the story, you may have grasped at the first convenient idea, but is it something that would really happen? A great ending often feels like an inevitable ending.

- Make sure all story threads are woven together snugly. A great ending is about satisfying the reader. Leaving loose ends—even little ones—can make a reader feel grumpy.

THIRTY-TWO

#OuchCriticism!

After I finish writing this book, I am going to send it to my literary agent. She'll read it and tell me what she thinks. This is what my email to her will look like:

Hi Alice.
I finally finished #STUCK! Phew, that took longer than I thought it would! I hope it's worth the wait. I'm attaching it below. Give it a read and let me know what you think.
XXOO Ellen

Now, I really do want to hear what she honestly thinks. But I also want her to 100% love it. I want her to love it so much that she won't want me to change a thing.

That's my Ego talking.

Thankfully, I also have a Professional Writer voice. The Professional Writer voice says, "Yes, of course I want you to love this book, Alice. But I also want this book to be so good that writers all over the world will want to keep it nearby whenever they're writing. I want them to open it up whenever they feel stuck and I want it to help them move past all those frustrating writing problems. Oh, and I also want it to be entertaining. That's why you have to let me know which parts of this book aren't working or are boring or are awkward or are just plain terrible. I'll listen. I won't like to hear the bad stuff, but I'll listen and if I agree, I'll go back and revise it."

Alice will tell me what she thinks about this book, and because I trust her as a reader and a human being (this is key when you are looking for feedback), I will most likely go back and revise the parts she thinks need revising. No drama. No tears. Although I've put my heart and soul into the writing of this book, this book is not me. And your story is not you.

 tuckbuster

Who Should Give Me Feedback?

When your parents sent you to summer camp, they didn't just plop you down at an abandoned nuclear power plant where the counselors all had criminal records and the daily activities included shooting rats with a BB gun (please tell me they didn't!). No, they probably did some research, asked around, and thought hard about which camp would be a good fit for you. Treat your story in the same way. When you are finding a person to give you feedback, it's smart to be picky. Here are some things to think about:

- Does your reader read a lot? Even better, do they write a lot? You want to give your story to someone who understands how stories work and can tease out the problem spots.

- Will your reader give you honest feedback? If they are too afraid to hurt your feelings, they might just give you a lot of sweet talk. That's always nice—we all want people to love our work—but ultimately, it's not very helpful.

- Does your reader have your best interests at heart? If you suspect they don't, proceed with caution! You are putting yourself in a vulnerable position when you hand your story to someone. It's all too easy for them to undermine you by tearing apart your work.

- If you know several people who would be good readers, even better! It's helpful to have more than one reader weigh in.

- Close friends and family are not always the best readers for your work. Sorry. They might be too worried about hurting your feelings to give you an honest critique. If you do ask them to read it, make sure to tell them to be brutally honest. Well . . . maybe just honest.

THIRTY-THREE

#Rejection

Professional writers may not look any different than other people but we are. We have an extra layer of skin that is as tough as Kevlar. It helps to protect us from harsh criticism, rejection letters, and nasty reviews on Amazon. That's not to say that these things don't hurt us—they do, oh, they do! But we're able to recover and move on more quickly than the average person.

How To Grow Bulletproof Skin

Are we born with bulletproof skin? Nope. We grow it over the years, layer by layer. Whenever you encounter criticism and rejection and you don't lose your cool, you are growing a new layer. Even if you don't become a professional writer, bulletproof skin will help you handle unkind comments and difficult relationships. It will give you resilience. You'll take a hit and keep on going. Or as an old Japanese proverb says, "Fall seven times, stand up eight"

When Receiving Feedback . . . Zip It!

When someone is giving you feedback on your story, it's always tempting to jump in and defend your work, as in, "But you don't understand the ending! I meant [fill in the blank]."

Defending your work probably won't change the person's view of it, and besides, writers can't be standing behind all their readers to explain the story. If there is something that your reader doesn't understand unless you explain it to them, it's probably because you haven't made it clear enough in the story (or it might be because the reader just didn't get it. I'll talk about that in a minute).

Here's what you do while receiving feedback:

BE QUIET AND JUST LISTEN. It's hard, I know, but zip it. If you must say something it should be "Ah ha" or "I get what you're saying."

After they are done, *and only after they are done,* you can ask questions. Not defend, ask. This is to help you figure out what, if anything, needs to be revised. For instance, if your reader says that they didn't believe your two characters would fall in love, you can ask your reader why. Was the chemistry just not there, or was it that the situation made a love-match unlikely, or did one character do something or say something that would make a relationship a no-go? Or maybe it's something else. Then ask your reader if they have any suggestions as to how it to fix the problem.

Take notes. Not only will this help you to remember what your reader says, it's also a handy trick that defense lawyers have their clients do during a trial. It gives you something to focus on when you are in the "hot seat."

Say "Thank you." Even if the only thing they really liked about your story was the title, say "Thank you." They took the time to read your work and to think about it, and they deserve to be thanked. Besides, it will help you grow yet another layer of bulletproof skin.

What if I Don't Agree With The Feedback?

You will definitely get feedback with which you don't agree. In fact, I'll bet you won't agree with 90% of the feedback you get . . . not at first, anyway. Listen to what the person is saying, even if you have to grit your teeth. Even if the whole time you are thinking, "Sheesh, you so are dumb! Why don't you understand that the ending is meant to be unclear!"

After you have let the feedback settle in for a day, you may discover that the ending to the story really *is* unclear. And not in a good way. And you may decide you had better change it. Or, after you have let the feedback settle for a day, you might decide that you still want the ending to be unclear. And that's fine too.

Use It Or Scrap It?

Now . . . there will be feedback that is *not* useful. It takes some practice to figure out which suggestions you should use and which you shouldn't. Here are some tips on what to look for:

The best feedback is specific. It's one thing to say, "I didn't like the main character." That might just be your reader's personal bias. Maybe they don't like sporty characters or characters with a cynical outlook on life. However, if your reader explains why they didn't connect with the main character—maybe the character felt cartoonish or didn't have any defining personality traits—that's useful feedback. You can work with that. If your reader was not specific, ask them for more information. If their answer is still too vague, then you might need to ignore the feedback.

Is your reader's preference for a certain style or genre influencing their feedback? Did they not like your use of a magic portal in a Porta Potty because they aren't fans of fantasy stories or because they didn't think the description of the magic portal was detailed enough? Or too gross? Or did the magic portal save the character in a way that seemed too convenient? Here again, the more specific the feedback, the better the feedback.

Was the feedback mean spirited? Did it get personal? If so, scrap it.

. . .

*T*ry it out.

You can do a revision incorporating the feedback, and if the story suddenly falls flat or if you lose interest in it, then that feedback is not for you. After a while, you might instinctually know which feedback is useful and which isn't. Personally, I'll feel a resistance in the pit of my stomach when I contemplate feedback that won't work for the story.

#*S*tuckbusters

Here are a few things that might help take the sting out of criticism:

- Start working on a new story when you give in your first one for feedback. If you are excited and immersed in a new story, you'll be able to be more objective and unemotional about hearing the feedback for your older story.

- As you hear the feedback, remember this: You don't have to change a thing in your story. Just because someone thinks the story is too dark, doesn't mean they are right. Keeping this in mind will help break your resistance to hearing the feedback.

- I use the "Rule of Three" when figuring out if I should use feedback and revise. If three people point out the same problematic issue in my book, I will usually go back and revise it.

- Right at the start, give your reader some guidance as to what will be most helpful to you. For instance, you can tell them that you want to know which parts feel too slow or which parts are confusing. You can ask them if they think the characters feel authentic. You might want to know if your descriptions are clear enough. With a little direction, your reader's feedback will be more on target.

Think about joining a writers' group. If there aren't any around, you can start one. If you are starting a writing group, it's always a good idea to consider a few things:

- How many people will be in the group? If there are too many, it will be hard for everyone to share their work; too few and it might not be helpful. I find around 5 to 8 members is a good number, although I once had a great writer's group with just three members.

- It's also a good idea for members to have similar levels of commitment. If you are a serious short story writer or novelist but most of the other people in the group just like to do a little journaling, the group might not be a fit for you.

- Is there a page limit on the length of the stories the group will review? You don't want to overwhelm each other.

- How will critiques work? Will you just tell each other what was working in the pieces or will you be digging in more deeply? If you are giving each other more thorough critiques, you might want to establish some etiquette rules, so you don't all wind up hating each other. For instance, it's often better to start with the positives before you point out the possible problems. And always, always be gentle and compassionate!

- You can also do "group writing" at the meetings. That means everyone works on their own pieces, or writing prompts (see #DIYWritingWorkshop), while you sit together. I actually love writing in a group. It feels so nice to be able to sit in silence with other people. Also, when you're stuck you can't just get up and raid the fridge or clean the toilet instead of writing (well, technically you could, but the others might think you were a weirdo, especially if you weren't in your own home).

THIRTY-FOUR

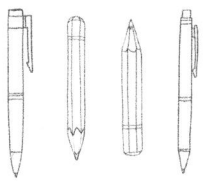

#Revision
_____

Whenever I finish writing a book, I triumphantly thump my finger against the Caps Lock key and type the two most delightful words in the English language: THE END.

Now I can kick back and relax. *Ahhh*. A little *People Magazine* action. A foot massage? Yes, thank you.

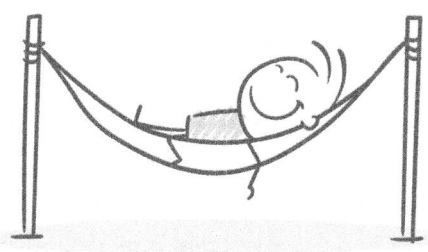

But after a day or two of reading about "Who wore it

better," a tiny voice in my head whispers, "Um, aren't you forgetting something, Ellen?"

That thing would be revision.

For a writer, "THE END" is never really the end. Oh, I suppose there might be a couple of writers who can whip out a flawless book without ever having to go back and revise it. If you meet one, let me know. I'm still looking.

Takesies-Backsies

Do you have to revise? No. You don't have to brush your teeth in the morning either, but your breath is going to stink and no one is going to want to talk to you. Similarly, a story that isn't polished, that is riddled with grammatical errors, holes in the plot, clunky word choices, etc., is not going to win you any fans. Worse than that, you are committing the cardinal sin of yanking readers out of your fictional world. They will suddenly frown at an exchange of dialogue that makes no sense, or they will have to go back and reread a section because they are confused. A sloppy story tells your readers that you don't care enough about it to get it right. If you don't care about your story, why on earth should they?

Listen, gang, writers are lucky—*lucky*, I tell you— to be able to revise. Think about singers who have one shot at hitting that high note, or stage actors who have to know all their lines. If they make a mistake, there are no takesies-backsies. We writers, on the other hand, have the luxury of do-overs . . . as many as we like.

Is it a pain to revise? Sometimes. But think of it this way: the hardest part is over. You have already finished the story! You've created something out of nothing! While you were writing the first draft, you may have had doubts about your plot, your characters, and your writing skills, yet you kept writing. Revision? It's a piece of cake compared to that. I'm not just pep-talking you here. Revision, like so many other things in life, (going to the gym, cleaning your room, apologizing to your aunt for that comment you made about her weird laugh) seems harder when you think about it than when you actually do it. And maybe I'm a nerd, but I find the revision process oddly enjoyable. It reminds me of that satisfaction you feel when working on a difficult jigsaw puzzle and finally snapping in those last few pieces. *Ahh*, done!

Now where's my *People* magazine?

#Stuckbusters

- Give yourself a day or two to relax and ready yourself for "story surgery."

- Start with the easiest changes first, then gradually work your way up to the harder stuff. This is a great way to handle "revision resistance." As you whip through the easy parts, you'll gain confidence (and realize how much your story can benefit from a few nips and tucks). By the time you get to the more challenging revisions, you'll be warmed up and ready to roll.

- Have one or two people whom you trust read your work. Ideally, they should be people who have your best interests at heart, are honest, and are sharp-eyed readers. That said, avoid giving your work to people who adore you so much that they wouldn't dream of saying anything negative about your work. (Yes, I love those people, too, but they won't be of much help to you in this case.)

- A quick tip for getting a helpful critique: Tell your readers what you are looking for. Be specific. For instance, ask them to mark any places in your story that are confusing or boring. Ask for feedback on your characters: Do their motives seem clear? Do they seem solid and real, or do they step out of character often? Ask if your characters interact in believable ways. You can also simply let your critique partner give their impressions freely. A good critique can be a goldmine for your revision!

- Revision has a way of bringing out the snarling rebel in writers, as in, "If people don't like this story, that's their problem!" I definitely used to feel like that when I was a younger writer. But writing is about connecting to your readers. It's about making them think and feel and wonder. I'm not saying that you should try to please everyone, but you want to write the best story you possibly can. If you want people to read your stories—and I'm assuming you do—you have to make it easier for them to fall in love with your work.

- Here are a few things you might want to think about when revising:

Have I left any loose threads?

Are any of my characters soggy or bland?

Are my characters consistent? Do their actions make sense?

Are there any holes in the plot?

Are my settings vivid enough?

Could some of my word choices be better?

Are there any words that I repeat too often or too closely together?

Is any of my dialogue unnecessary? Does it sound natural?

Does each scene have the power that I had intended?

Is there anything that is confusing? Boring?

Does the ending feel satisfying?

Check your spelling and grammar. It does make a difference. When I read stories with a lot of misspellings or poor grammar, I lose confidence in the writer.

- Finally, SAVE ALL YOUR DRAFTS!! I can't tell you how many times I revised the snot out of something and in the end decided that I liked an earlier draft best. Go figure.

THIRTY-FIVE

#TechTalk

Social media can be very helpful when you are struggling with a story.

Wait, what?

Did you think I was going to say social media was a massive time suck that turns your brain into pudding? Well, that can be true too. Still, I'm assuming that you are a sensible person who isn't spending every hour of the day taking selfies or swapping your face with a gerbil's.

Used the right way, social media can be a great tool when

you're stuck, especially if you have the right Followers or Friends or Worshipers or whatever. Imagine you are sitting alone in your bedroom, trying to figure out what a school librarian would wear on a date or how to describe the expression on someone's face when they've been caught in a lie. If you post the question, you might have hundreds of people stepping up to offer their thoughts. Yes, most of the suggestions will probably be ridiculous, but you might find one or three that will actually work. And even if they don't work, they might send your thoughts in a different direction that will ultimately lead you to the perfect solution.

I've seen many well-known authors post shout-outs like this, asking for help with names of real restaurants in Paris or to check in about plot points. It's not as thorough or reliable as having a good reader go through your story, but it can work in a pinch.

The Dumb Stuff

I know I don't even have to say this, because you already know it. But I'll say it anyway because I am not only a professional writer, I'm also a professional worrier. There's a lot of dumb stuff on social media. A LOT. It can eat up your time and suck out the best parts of your brain. If you spend too much time on social media, your creativity will tank and you will wind up with the attention span of a hummingbird. I know of what I speak, by the way. I've had periods of time where I spent far too much time on social media and my writing, and focus, suffered for it. As much as possible, use some self-control with social media. Limit the time you use it so that you are not mindlessly yakking and clicking and snapping your life away.

One other thing . . . be cautious on social media. Yes, I know you've heard this a million times before, but too bad. If

I don't say this, I will worry about you. There are loads of people who are just plain mean or jealous and don't have your best interests at heart. Be smart. Be alert. Be careful.

Okay, I won't say another word on the subject. My lips are officially zipped.

Stuckbusters

Blogging

I like to think of blogging as the "mudroom" of fiction writing. Imagine you are walking home after a long day. The streets are busy, noisy and freezing cold. Finally, you reach your house, open the door and walk into the mudroom. *Ahhh.* You let the outside world drop away. You take off your coat and boots. Maybe you dump your backpack or bag in the floor. The mudroom is chilly but it's a whole lot warmer than the world outside. You can still hear the street noise but it's muffled. Now you're ready to walk deeper into the house's interior.

If you find yourself nervous about starting a new story or you are stuck in procrastination mode, blogging can be an excellent way to ease yourself into fiction writing. It's an entry way, a mudroom to the interior world of your imagination.

Maybe you can simply write daily reflections. Or you can write about something you love to do, or know a lot about. If your friends are always asking you for advice about relationships, write about that. If politics is your passion, have at it. If you sculpt things out of beef jerky, well . . . yeah, why not, write about beef-jerky sculpting.

Why is writing a blog post such a good way to warm up for your fiction writing? Because it helps you write in a non-intimidating way. Writing a 300-word post on trend spotting is much less overwhelming than writing something much longer. Also, you are probably writing on a topic that you know well. That's nowhere near as scary as creating worlds and characters out of thin air. I find that after I finish a blog post, I am braver about dipping back into a story in which I've been stuck.

Another thing that I love about blog posts is that a writer can experience the sensation of actually finishing a piece of writing. I know many writers who have started dozens of stories but have never finished a single one. Finishing a piece of writing feels very different from all other aspects of writing. You get this incredible sense of satisfaction. It builds your confidence as a writer, and it propels you onward to your next piece of writing. It also allows you to experience how powerful the act of revision can be. While you might know that you can always revise your story once you finish, actually doing it and seeing how much better you can make your story once it is complete is a major eye opener.

Finally, blogging also satisfies that urge to publish, share your work and possibly even have a fan base. Who knows, maybe you'll discover a whole underground community of beef-jerky sculptors.

Fan Fiction

A while back, I asked a teen writer I know if she had been working on something. "Not really," she said. She paused, looking embarrassed, then added, "I mean, it's just fan fiction." She actually glanced around the room to see if anyone had overheard.

Why all the secrecy? I wondered.

As far as I'm concerned, fan fiction speaks to the heart of why we write. Because it's fun. Because we are fascinated by certain characters, maybe a little obsessed by them. We want to see what they will do next. What would happen if he didn't die in the car accident? What if she wound up dating the guy at the coffee shop?

I guess some people might think of fan fiction as a form of copying, but we all learn by imitation. Mimicking another writer's style or using their story to launch one of your own is a perfectly legitimate way to learn the craft.

If you post your fan fiction, steel yourself for feedback. You may get rave reviews all around. But you also may get some negative reviews as well. Some of the negative reviews will actually contain suggestions you can use, so yay. There will be other comments that are deliberately meant to be soul crushers.

Have you ever seen the Muppet movies? There are these cranky old puppets named Statler and Waldorf, who sit up in the balcony and snarl nasty comments about the other Muppets. There are a lot of Statler and Waldorfs online, so be prepared. You can generally spot them quite easily, since they have not one single good thing to say about most people's work. Also—and I don't know why this—soul crushers' grammar tends to stink.

Writing Software and Writing Apps

There are loads of these things. Some of them are decent and some of them are useless. Do I use any of them? Well, I've certainly tried out my share. The only software I have used more than once is Scrivener. It did help me to organize my work, though it wasn't absolutely necessary.

For the most part, I bought these software programs and apps because I was stuck and feeling desperate. I thought,

"*Hmm*, that app might be just the thing I need to get me past this rough patch." Did they help? In a way . . . while I was trying to figure out how to use them, they distracted me from feeling stuck and desperate.

Ultimately, all the apps and software in the world are no substitute for the writer's most basic tools: a hefty amount of perseverance.

THIRTY-SIX

#BestJobsForWriters

There are lots of great reasons to write fiction, but getting rich just isn't one of them. It often takes years for a fiction writer to be able to earn a decent —and in many cases, not-so-decent—living doing what they love. It took me over a decade, during which time I groomed dogs, was a receptionist at Ralph Lauren (every week I had to purchase twelve, blemish-free lemons and arrange them in a pyramid on the boss's coffee table), waited tables, did landscaping, taught art to little kids, and proofread books about the Royal British Navy. Yes, there are a handful of writers whose best-selling first novels have bought them their own private island, but frankly you have a better chance of getting hit in the head with an asteroid.

The bottom line is you will have to figure out a way to support yourself while you are writing fiction. So what sort of job is best? Certainly there are jobs in related fields, like technical writing, journalism, or teaching creative writing. For some fiction writers, these jobs are a good fit, while for others, writing-related jobs might sap their creative energy.

Brain Stamina

As a general rule, I think any job that allows you to go home after work and still have the energy to write is a good job for a fiction writer. Keep in mind that less isn't always more. A part-time job won't necessarily leave you with more energy than a nine-to-five job. Working the morning shift in a doughnut shop might drain your energy faster than a career as a defense attorney. Or it might be the other way around. If you are bored with your job, you are going to come home feeling like someone has poked a straw in your ear and slurped out your brain. Good luck working on your novel at the end of that kind of day. The only thing you are going to want to work on is a pint of Rocky Road ice cream. That's why, if at all possible, try to find a job that leaves your mind in decent working order at the end of the day.

For some people, that might mean a job which keeps you on your toes mentally. For other people, a job that demands intense mental exertion might leave their brains too fried to work on their novel; instead, a more physical job might be the ticket. The better you know yourself and your physical and mental stamina, the better shot you have at choosing a job that's compatible with writing.

$$$

Another thing to consider is money. You're going to need some. And since it will almost certainly be a while before you'll see any income from your writing, you have to ask yourself this:

How much do I like eating grilled cheese sandwiches for dinner?

Really, you need to be honest with yourself about money and how much of it you need in order to feel okay, and not cringe in terror every time you look at your bank statement. The whole starving artist thing is fine until you really are starving. I'm not saying that you need to become a Wall Street broker (unless, of course, you have a passion for it). It's just that when you are always stressed about money, it can be hard to focus and be creative. If you are the kind of person who needs to keep their credit card warm with plenty of daily swipings, then you might consider a job that will keep your bank account plump.

When I first started writing, I chose to avoid a high-powered career because I was nervous it would zap my writing energy. Since I am a low-maintenance sort of person, I figured I didn't need to make a ton of money. Instead, I patched together a bunch of odd jobs to keep myself afloat until my writing career took off. The jobs didn't pay very well, but they brought in enough money to cover my bills. For me, having the time and energy to write was more satisfying than buying expensive shoes or going to fancy restaurants. But that's a life choice, and it's definitely not for everyone.

Even the jobs you hate may help you as a writer. After all, it was during a stint as a high school janitor that Stephen King was inspired to write *Carrie*. In order to write well you need to be engaged with the world around you, so maybe it's a good thing that writers are forced to step away from their stories and rustle up some cash. If I had been sitting at home all day typing, instead of waiting tables, I never would have met Cambodian refugees or aspiring stand-up comedians. Your job may actually feed your creativity as well as your belly.

THIRTY-SEVEN

#GettingPublished

I'm breaking a promise by including this section. I promised myself that I would absolutely not write a section about getting published. Of course, I'm all for books getting published. You wouldn't be reading this book now if I wasn't. It's just that I think young (and not-so-young) writers are often obsessed with getting published before they're ready. It's like being so hungry that you eat the fried chicken before it's fully cooked. It may satisfy your immediate hunger but ultimately it's not super great for you. Instead, the focus should be squarely on becoming a good writer. Possibly even a great one.

That can take a while.

However, since the #1 question that young writers ask me is, "How can I get my book published?" I guess I'd better answer it as best as I can.

By the way, I'm not going to address self-publishing, although I know several people who have done quite well with it. Still, I don't have a ton of personal experience with it, so I feel like it wouldn't be fair to shoot my mouth off on the topic.

Buffed and Polished

First things first . . . finish the book completely. Editors and literary agents won't look at an unfinished manuscript of a writer who has never been published before. You may have completed seven of the most brilliant chapters that have ever been written in the history of mankind, but editors still won't make you an offer. They want to see that you have the staying power to finish the entire manuscript. They want to know that your characters can capture a reader's interest well into the book, and that the storyline maintains its momentum and holds together until the very last sentence.

Once your manuscript is completely finished, congratulations! You are about halfway done. Now you have to revise it. It's a rare writer who can get a story just right on the first draft. In fact, I haven't yet met a single writer who can. The competition to publish is fierce. Editors are usually drowning in manuscript submissions. That means your manuscript needs to be buffed and polished to perfection—or as close to it as possible—if you want it to catch an editor's eye.

Literary Agents

I'm a big believer in writers having literary agents, especially if you want to get published at a mainstream publishing house. A literary agent helps to sell your book, negotiate contracts and generally watch your back. In return they receive (usually) a 15% commission on everything you get paid. You should avoid agents who ask to be paid up front (which they sometimes call a "reading fee") or if they are asking for more than a 15% commission.

A good agent is a writer's best friend in the business. Why? Because your agent will know which publishing houses and editors would be a good fit for your manuscript.

More importantly, the editors know and (hopefully) trust your agent. A manuscript that is sent to an editor by a reputable literary agent is much more likely to be read than one that is sent to an editor by the author. That's not to say that it's impossible for an author to get published if they don't have an agent. It does happen, but the odds are not "ever in your favor."

Your agent knows how to negotiate the best deal for you. I mean, it's possible that you are a whiz at contract negotiations. If you are, go for it. However, most writers I know, myself included, are not. Of course, you do want to educate yourself as much as possible about contracts, but contract negotiations are often lengthy and complicated, and I'd rather spend my time writing my next novel.

Agents are also a buffer between you and the publishing world. They can tactfully iron out problems you might be having with your editor or your publicist. They can shield you from some of the more unkind rejections. They can also be the first readers of your manuscript. Agents are often very savvy readers, and they can help you to shape your book so that it will be as publishable as possible.

So, how does a writer get an agent?

There are some online sites that list literary agencies by

genre so that you can figure out which ones would be right for your work. Once you've chosen some agents that look like a good fit, read their submission guidelines and write a query letter. A query letter is a brief letter that tells an agent about your work and yourself. It's basically a way to entice the agent so that they ask to see your work.

Check out the *Writer's Digest* website for some great advice on finding literary agents and writing query letters.

After you've sent off your query letter, try to forget about it. Work on another story. Take up archery. Start a blog. Learn Krav Maga. Just don't dwell on it because it can take agents a long time to get back to you. Like months sometimes.

Be prepared for rejection. Not to be a downer here, but rejection is going to happen, so brace yourself. Some rejections will come with an explanation as to why the agent is not interested in seeing your manuscript. Many won't. There are lots of ways to handle rejection. You can:

1. Sit in the bathroom and sob.

2. Resolve never to write another word again.

3. Decide that the person who rejected you was a world-class knucklehead.

4. Think about why your book was rejected, especially if the agent gave you an explanation. Then you can decide whether or not to revise your query letter or rethink your manuscript.

5. Send out your query to a new agent and get on with your life.

Having tried all of the above, I recommend options 4 and

5. Because eventually someone is going to need to get into that bathroom.

The Road To Getting Published

You, or your agent if you have one, send your manuscript to an editor, or several different editors.

You wait.

You wait some more.

You will probably get a rejection or two. Or thirty.

If an editor likes your manuscript, they will make an offer. That means $$$. Or more likely $.

You or your agent will negotiate a contract. That contract will cover royalties, foreign rights, subsidiary rights, among other things. Negotiating and finalizing a contract usually takes several months, so you probably won't be seeing any money coming in for a while. Typically, you don't get all the money at once either. You might get a percentage of the payment once you sign the contract and another percentage once you have revised the manuscript to your editor's satisfaction. Sometimes the payment is broken into three allotments in which the final portion is paid after your book is published.

How much money will you make on your first book? It's really impossible to say. It all depends on the publishing company, the genre in which you are writing, if the editors suspect your book is going to be a runaway bestseller, etc. For a point of reference—there were definitely many years in which I made more money as a waitress than I did as a writer.

Once you have a published or soon-to-be-published book under your belt, you might get an advance to write another book. That means you'll be paid a percentage of the payment for your second novel before you have even written a word.

#Writers911

Sweet, right? Except, uh oh, guess what? Now you have a deadline. And that's a whole 'nother ball of wax.

Once you've signed your contract, your editor will send you their suggestions for changes they'd like to see in your manuscript. Sometimes you will agree with these changes. Sometimes you won't. You do not have to make all the changes that your editor suggests. However, even if you don't agree with an editor's suggested changes, don't rule them out right away. Give them a little time to sink in. The editor might be on to something. Or not. If you decide you do not want to use their suggestions, let them know why. Not only is it the polite thing to do, but it will also help you to be extra clear on why you want to keep things as they are.

Several months before your book's publication date (which is usually about a year to a year and a half after your manuscript is accepted), your publisher will send ARCs (Advanced Reader Copies) of your book to reviewers. They may also assign a publicist to you who will help you to spread the word about your book, as well as possibly booking some events. If you are active on social media, that helps. More and more, publishers rely on authors to publicize their own books, so being social media savvy is a big plus.

A few weeks before your book is published, the reviews start coming in. This can be pretty stressful. If you're lucky, all the reviews will be glowing. Probably, though, you will get some reviews that are stinkers. For some reason, even if you get a dozen great reviews, it's the one bad review that really sticks in your mind.

Some writers refuse to read any reviews at all—good or bad. That's smart. Unfortunately, I don't possess that much self-control, which means I get my heart squished like a cherry tomato every now and then. This is one reason I start working on my next book as soon as I finish my first one. A bad review feels less devastating if you have another book in the works. Think about it this way: if you only have one friend and that friend decides they don't like you anymore, it's just the worst! But if you have a dozen friends, and one of those friends deserts you, it's much more bearable.

Yay, it's Pub Day! Your book's birthday! Now, I won't deny that it's pretty sweet to see your book on the shelves of a bookstore. It was surreal to see one of my books next to Philip Pullman's books (thank you, alphabetical order!). But I have to admit something. I've always found my books' publication day a little anticlimactic. It seems like there should be fireworks and parties and champagne corks popping, but it's generally not very different from any other day. Oh, there may be a few congratulatory Tweets. Some nice Facebook posts. An email from my editor and my agent. But otherwise, pretty ordinary.

Honestly, the best day in the whole process is the day I finally finish a book, and I mean really finish it, including revisions. When I type "The End" and actually mean it. Nothing compares to that day. Nothing.

THIRTY-EIGHT

#DIYWritingWorkshop

I often use writing prompts when I'm stuck. They flex my imagination and remind me that writing is supposed to be fun.

Below are a few writing prompts that you can use on your own or with a group. Speaking of groups, you might consider either joining or starting a writing club. You can use prompts like the ones below or individually work on stories that you've already started.

The club can be structured any way you like. You could start with writing prompts, then people could share pieces of writing they've been working on, or vice versa. You could even do a group story.

As far as critiquing each other's work, I'm a firm believer in keeping things positive for works-in-progress. Club members could comment on what they enjoyed most about each other's stories—which scenes worked the best, which characters popped, what parts of the storyline were most intriguing. The point is to keep each other motivated enough to get to the finish line. After the first draft is done, then the group can give the author a more thorough critique.

Below are some of my favorite writing games to help light up your imagination . . .

Mystery Package

Write a story in which there is a knock on your character's door. When they answer it, no one's there. Instead they find a box. Inside the box there is (choose one of the following objects: a key; an old dog collar; a woman's shoe; a note saying "Why did you do it?").

Change of Heart

Write a story in which your character starts out desperately wanting one thing, but winds up wanting the opposite thing in the end. For instance, a character might begin by wanting to reconnect to an old friend but by the end of the story never wants to see that same friend again.

Spill It

Pair up with a partner. Using a single sheet of paper passed back and forth, create a written conversation in which one person has a secret and the other person is trying to persuade the first person to spill the beans. Establish your character before you begin and try to keep your character's voice authentic and consistent throughout the conversation.

R.I.P.

I'm fascinated by obituaries. No, I'm not being ghoulish. It's just that obituaries often tell stories of remarkable people, distilling their lives into a few paragraphs. Have a look at a few. The *New York Times* has excellent ones. Chances are you'll find some fascinating story ideas in there.

Clothes Make The Character

Describe your character's clothes, all of them: shoes, socks, underwear, pants. Describe the brand, the color, the condition. Are the clothes wrinkled, ironed crisply, frayed? Are there stains? What kind? Examining your character's clothes can reveal so much about their lives—what they value, how they view themselves, their lifestyle, etc.

Backpack Challenge 1

Empty your backpack (or handbag or messenger bag or whatever you use to lug your stuff around). All of it, even the candy wrappers and the broken hair bands.

Look at all the items in there and write one of the following:

1. A horror story about an item in your backpack.

2. A love story between two items in your backpack.

3. A story in which one of the items in your backpack has magical properties.

Backpack Challenge 2

Your character has a secret that they keep in their backpack. It can be a letter, an object, a living creature, etc. Think about why this secret is important to your character and what the consequences are if the secret is revealed. Now write a story in which your character has to struggle to keep their secret away from prying eyes.

Backpack Challenge 3 (or Dystopian Backpack Challenge)

As a rite of passage on their planet, all teens are dropped off on an island where they have to survive for a month on their own. The only thing they are given is a backpack containing five items. The island is home to several savage beasts, bouts of torrential rainfall, and some hostile villagers who will take the teens prisoner if they catch them.

1. Decide what's in the backpack. Each item should be essential to survival.

2. Draw a map of the island. Include the areas where the beasts live, the village, water sources, possible food sources, places to find shelter, any unusual terrain (i.e., poisonous-gas swamps, deadly cliffs, rivers with deadly currents or man-eating creatures, etc.).

3. Write a story in which one of those items in the backpack is taken or lost. Your character cannot survive without it. Will they try to retrieve that item? Will they figure out an alternative to that item? Will they attempt to befriend a villager and ask for help? Or will they find another solution?

Lost and Found

Your character had found a magical item (it can be anything—a ring, a wand, a living creature, a pair of glasses, etc.) along with an instruction manual. The manual is old and some of the pages are missing. Your character has to figure out how the magical object works.

Lists

These lists can help you get to the heart of the things you care about most and can help spark story ideas. Challenge yourself to write at least 20 items for each list:
1. Write a list of the things you don't remember.
2. Write a list of the things that you are obsessed with.
3. Write a list of things that scare you.

The Secret Room

There is a hidden room in a house. Write a story or scene in which your character finds a way in. What's in there? Why has the room been kept hidden?

Wait, What Just Happened?

Choose a photo and write about what happened right before or right after the photo was taken.

Headliners

You know those headlines on magazine covers? The ones that try to entice you to buy the magazine? Well, they can make great openings for a story. You can turn them into a line of dialogue, or add on to them, or just use them as a title for your story.

Here are a few of them I just randomly chose out of my stack of old magazines:

Dad, Prince, and Me
The World is Bigger Than We Imagine
Jet Set Selfies
There's A New Blonde in Town
Meddlers, Nags and Other Annoying People
Welcome to the Revolution
She's Just Wild About Harry
The Mystery of the Megaliths

THIRTY-NINE

#Top10WritingTips

Okay, we all love Top 10 Lists, so . . .

TOP 10 WRITING TIPS

1. Write every day.

2. Read. Read voraciously. Read great books, then read them again to figure out why they are so great. Read lousy books and figure out why they are so lousy. Don't forget to read the classics too. Reading will give you an ear for language that is impossible to develop otherwise.

3. Remember, no one gets a story right the first time around. First drafts are almost always lousy. Revision is your best friend.

4. If you get stuck, don't despair. It's normal. Reread this book or just flip to #Writers911

5. Find some writer friends. Writing can sometimes be lonely and frustrating, so it's great to have friends who not only understand, but are also happy to read your work and offer insights. And of course, you'll do the same for them.

6. Find a writing partner. (see #WritingPartners) This is truly one of the most helpful things a writer can do. It holds you accountable and helps you to finish your story. Plus, it's just way more fun.

7. Take walks when you are stuck. Walking and thinking oils up your brain and helps it to churn out those great ideas again.

8. Limit your screen time. Seriously, it affects your ability to focus and, in my experience, it messes with your creativity.

9. Do other things besides writing. Join a whale rescue club, take photos of people's tongues, learn how to do CPR or read Tarot cards or play the bagpipes. It will make you a more interesting and interested person. Plus, everything you do and learn feeds into your writing anyway. It's hard to come up with story ideas and create great characters if all you ever do is write.

10 Have fun for goodness sakes! That's why you started writing in the first place.

FORTY

#Writers911!

When you are feeling hopelessly stuck and need a quick fix, unpack these emergency #Stuck-busters.

- **Take a walk.** Walking and thinking boosts your imagination in the most mysterious way. Whenever I'm stuck, taking a walk with my dogs is my go-to solution. Ninety percent of the time, I'll come back with an idea that will jumpstart by stalled-out brain.

- **Soak the Beans.** I've received lots of good advice over the years, but one of my favorites came from my friend, the brilliant Megan Shull (author of YA novels *The Swap* and *Bounce*). She says that when she gets stuck, she will "soak the beans." What does that mean exactly? Well I know most people buy their beans in a can. But if you buy dry beans, you have to soak them in water for many hours in order to get them ready to cook up nicely. I've tried it. It takes a whopping amount of patience. When Megan gets stuck on a story, she stops trying to write. Just for a day or two. She lets her ideas "soak." She might read a book, go for a run, see a friend. After that she'll sit back down and start writing again. Often she'll come back to her story with fresh ideas—her creative "beans" are ready and her story will start simmering away.

- *Shhhh!* Do something in silence. Take a shower. Shoot hoops. Knit. Get busy with a coloring book (I love those things). Do your nails. Floss your teeth. Take photos. Don't turn on the TV. Don't go on the Internet. Don't look at your phone. Don't talk on the phone. The idea here is that you are shifting the focus off of your stuck story, but at the same time you're leaving a quiet space for a solution to sidle up and surprise you.

- **Helpline.** Phone a friend, preferably one who either writes or reads a lot. Tell them what you are struggling with and see if they have any thoughts. Even if their solutions aren't quite right for you, hearing a fresh perspective on your story can redirect your imagination.

- **New View.** Change the point-of-view. Sometimes just switching from third person to first person or vice versa can send your shipwrecked story back out to sea again.

- **Reconnect with the Rebels.** Are you sure that your characters' actions and decisions in your story are true to their nature? Or did you have them do certain things because you wanted the story to go a particular way? If you make your characters do things that they really wouldn't do, they will "rebel." They will dig in their heels and make your story stall out. If you suspect you've stopped listening to your characters, have another chat with them. Check in. Make sure you remember what your character wants more than anything in the world. It may be that you need to backtrack in your storyline and have a character make a different decision or take a different action. Once you get your characters breathing again, they will stop rebelling and help your story to move forward.

- **Hush-Hush.** Consider adding a secret. This may create an extra dimension to your character that will get your story going again. A word of warning though, don't force it into the plot. It has to feel natural. It has to make sense for the character.

- **Switch Writing Tools.** If you are writing on a computer, write by hand. If you're writing by hand, try writing on a computer. Use a different color pen or buy yourself a new notebook. I know it seems silly but even a little change like this can ease you out of a slump.

- **Move Along.** If you are stuck because you keep rewriting a chapter and can't seem to move past it, it can feel like that movie *Groundhog Day*. Remind yourself that it's fine if the chapter isn't perfect. Guess what? That's what revision is for. You can give yourself time limits for each chapter. For instance, you can allot yourself two days for a chapter before you move onto the next one.

- **Play Games.** Try some writing games like the ones listed in #DIYWritingWorkshop. Writing just for the fun of it will oil up those rusty gears in your imagination and get things moving again.

- **Remember** why you started writing in the first place. You write to experience a life that isn't your own, to feel what it's like to be a warrior or a British spy or an heiress. You write in order to travel places—whether it's Paris or a forbidden wasteland or a post-apocalyptic town in New Jersey. You write to make sense of the world or to escape the world or to laugh at the world. You write to share the dazzling visions in your head with other people. You write because when you finally type THE END—and you really mean it—it is one of the most satisfying feelings you'll ever experience.

THE END
Yup. That feels great.

spilling ink

A YOUNG WRITER'S HANDBOOK

BY ANNE MAZER
AND ELLEN POTTER
ILLUSTRATED BY
MATT PHELAN

About the Author

Ellen Potter is the author of more than 20 award-winning novels for children and young adults, including *Olivia Kidney, Slob, Big Foot and Little Foot, Piper Green and The Fairy Tree, The Humming Room, Pish Posh,* and *The Kneebone Boy.* Several of her books have been chosen by New York Public Library as a Best 100 Books for Children, and have appeared on numerous State Reading Lists.

Her non-fiction writing guide, *Spilling Ink, A Young Writer's Handbook,* co-authored with Anne Mazer, was also chosen by New York Public Library's as a Best 100 Books for Children, and was a Children's Literature Assembly 2011 Notable Book.

Ellen lives in Upstate New York with her family.
Website: https://www.ellenpotter.com

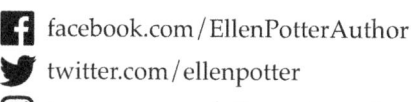

facebook.com/EllenPotterAuthor
twitter.com/ellenpotter
instagram.com/ellenpotterauthor

Also by Ellen Potter

Spilling Ink, A Young Writer's Handbook
SLOB
The Kneebone Boy
The Humming Room
Pish Posh
Olivia Kidney

Made in the USA
Coppell, TX
26 February 2021